*This Prayer Book
is a gift for / belongs to:*

_____

❦

If lost, please contact below to return to owner:

Email: _____

Text/SMS: _____

GET PRAYERS ANSWERED
MY PRAYER JOURNAL OF CONVERSATIONS WITH HEAVEN

STEVE CIOCCOLANTI

DISCOVER MEDIA

Get Prayers Answered: My Prayer Journal of Conversations with Heaven

Published by Discover Media www.discover.org.au

Copyright © 2024 by Steve Cioccolanti. All rights reserved.

No part of this book may be reproduced in any form, except for the use of brief quotations in a book review. Unless otherwise noted, all Scripture quotations are taken from New King James Version of the Bible. Copyright © 1979, 1980, 1982. Used by permission of Thomas Nelson, Inc., Publishers.

Scriptures taken from other versions are marked as below and used by permission:

(AKJ) American KJV. Used by permission of Cambridge University Press.

(AMPC) Amplified Bible, Classic Edition. Copyright © 1954, 1958, 1962, 1964, 1965, 1987 by The Lockman Foundation.

(CEB) Common English Bible (CEB). Copyright © 2011 by Common English Bible.

(CEV) Contemporary English Version. Copyright © 1995 by American Bible Society.

(CSB) The Christian Standard Bible. Copyright © 2017 by Holman Bible Publishers.

(God's Word)

(GNT) Good News Translation® (Today's English Version, Second Edition) © 1992 American Bible Society.

(HCSB) Holman Christian Standard Bible. Copyright © 1999, 2000, 2002, 2003, 2009 by Holman Bible Publishers.

(ISV) International Standard Version. Copyright © 1995-2014 by ISV Foundation. Used by permission of Davidson Press, LLC.

(KJ21) 21st Century King James Version. Copyright © 1994 by Deuel Enterprises, Inc.

(MEV) Modern English Version. Copyright © 2014 by Military Bible Association. Published and distributed by Charisma House.

(NET) New English Translation or NET Bible®. Copyright ©1996-2017 by Biblical Studies Press.

(NLT) New Living Translation, copyright © 1996, 2004, 2015 by Tyndale House Foundation. Used by permission of Tyndale House Publishers, Inc.

Paperback ISBN 978-1-962907-06-4 | Hardback ISBN 978-1-962907-08-8 | E-book ISBN 978-1-962907-07-1

Cover design by *Selena Sok*.

Printed in the U.S.A.

CONTENTS

Why I Wrote This Book 7

1. How to Use This Book 11
2. Basics of Prayer 15
3. People I Pray for 18
4. 6 Steps to Save Your Family 25
5. Aging 29
6. Ancient Prayers 32
7. Apostles' Creed 34
8. Assassination 37
9. Avenge Me 41
10. Books 46
11. Children 49
12. Church 55
13. Church Growth 57
14. Church Property 64
15. Court 66
16. Deliverance 72
17. Difficult People 77
18. Election 80
19. Emotions 82
20. Enemies 85
21. Evangelism 91
22. Family 95
23. Famine 98
24. Favor 100
25. Future 104
26. Goals & Priorities 108
27. Grace 116
28. Healing 119
29. Home Dedication 126
30. Houses to the Godly 130
31. Husband 133
32. Jobs & Opportunities 138
33. Joy 141
34. Justice 143
35. Kindness 149
36. Lawsuits & Legal Battles 153

37. Leader's Prayer	158
38. Lord's Prayer	161
39. Love	162
40. Miracles	165
41. Morning Praise	168
42. Nation	171
43. New Year	174
44. Pastors	180
45. Praise	182
46. Pregnancy	185
47. Pride	187
48. Protection	189
49. Prophet's Prayer	193
50. Psalm 23	196
51. Psalms	197
52. Questions	203
53. Revival	205
54. Sabbath Blessing	209
55. Sexual Purity	213
56. Sleep	217
57. Soul-winning	221
58. Studies	224
59. Temptation	228
60. War	230
61. Warfare Prayer	234
62. Wealth	238
63. Wife	243
64. Wisdom	247
65. World	251
66. Worship	254
Meet Steve Cioccolanti	259

WHY I WROTE THIS BOOK

This book contains 30 years of prayers that were answered. This is how I prayed. Sometimes God answered me within a minute. Sometimes it took 10 years for the answer to appear, but it always came. I never gave up. I never changed my prayer or repeated my request. I asked once, then thanked God. I believe there is a way to pray that brings success.

When others prayed in a similar way, sometimes exactly the same way word-for-word, they reported a similar success to mine.

I share this book with you because I believe the greatest motivator to living a Christian life is answered prayer. It's the proof we serve a living, caring God who keeps His Word.

Conversely, people have lost faith mainly over not getting answers to their prayers. Atheists are not people who don't believe in God; atheists are people who blame God. I've never had a conversation with an atheist who did not eventually reveal their question about unanswered prayer. Rather than humbling themselves to admit they didn't know something, they got emotional and angry.

They blamed God even though they have the power and responsibility to learn and obey the basic principles of prayer laid out in the Bible. There is a way that works. There are a thousand ways that don't work, too.

WHY I WROTE THIS BOOK

My aim is to help you find the right way and avert the common mistakes people make, especially ones picked up as a child or done out of desperation as an adult.

JAMES 1:5-8

5 If any of you lacks WISDOM, let him ask of God, who gives to all liberally and without reproach, and it will be given to him.
6 But let him ask in faith, with no doubting, for he who doubts is like a wave of the sea driven and tossed by the wind.
7 For let NOT that man suppose that he will RECEIVE anything from the Lord;
8 he is a double-minded man, UNSTABLE in all his ways.

WHAT I WANT TO LEARN MOST OUT OF THIS BOOK

_____
_____
_____
_____
_____
_____
_____
_____
_____
_____
_____
_____
_____
_____
_____
_____

1
HOW TO USE THIS BOOK

The first three chapters of this book are non-negotiable. They lay the foundation for getting prayers answered. Jesus told us how to pray in the Gospel of John. This type of prayer was not available under the Old Testament.

> **JOHN 16:23** (NKJV) "And in that day [meaning after Jesus died and rose again] you will ask Me nothing. Most assuredly, I say to you, whatever you ask the Father in My name He will give you."

The New Testament way to pray is to approach God the Father directly. Contrary to what you may have been taught, it's not acceptable to beg Mary or the saints to intercede on your behalf. Jesus said not to even ask Him. Jesus gave every child of God access to the Highest Authority in Heaven—God the Father.

Jesus instructed us to approach God the Father in the Name of God the Son. I intentionally use His Name "Jesus." I don't skirt around it and pray, "In Your Name." No, I like to say the Name that demons fear and Heaven hears: "Jesus."

The secret to my answered prayer is that I pray to the Father in the Name of Jesus. That means Jesus gave me His Power of Attorney. I am to speak what Jesus speaks. And God the Father will listen to me just as He listens to

Jesus. There is no need to go through another intermediary—Jesus is my only Mediator.

PRAYER REQUESTS

The most common prayer request I receive is for lost loved ones to be saved. It's so common that I did not put it under "Family," but as close to the top as possible, under the heading "**6 Steps to Save Your Family**." Please read the first three chapters, then skip around the other chapters as you feel led.

The second most common prayer request is for healing. I would study the "**Healing**" chapter. Of course, "Healing" will not be relevant to you if you're facing court or legal battles, in which case, you can head straight to the chapters titled "Court" and "Lawsuits & Legal Battles."

MY FAVORITES

The prayers I prayed most often have been for the "**Future**," the "**Nation**" and "**Warfare Prayer**," which I prayed daily for many years.

There are seasonal or periodic prayers. Every morning as a new Christian, I prayed the "**Morning Praise**." It was my own confession that has come true for me. Every week I try to have dinner with my children and pray the "**Sabbath Blessing**" over them.

At every New Year's Eve party, I print out my goals with Scriptures and sometimes inspiring pictures. My family and friends have seen me do this for thirty years. The New Year's Prayer changes from year to year, but you'll find a couple of models you can follow under "**New Year**."

THE MOST COMMON QUESTION

The most common question I get asked about prayer is, "*Why can't I pray for the same thing more than once?*" The short answer is that when you pray for the same thing 10 times, the first time was in faith, the next 9 times were in doubt. If you truly believed, you wouldn't ask again.

When you ask again, you no longer believe. I liken it to a child who repeatedly pesters a parent, checking if a parent is going to do something.

HOW TO USE THIS BOOK

The more times they ask, the more annoying it sounds. Annoying God...is *not* good practice.

Yes, there are prayers you can pray repeatedly. You can repeatedly praise God. You can repeatedly tell Him you love Him. Such prayers have nothing to do with asking in faith for a loved one to be saved, for your body to be healed, or for your court case to turn out favorably. They are not "prayers of faith."

Worship is an expression of gratitude. A child can tell a parent multiple times a day, "*I love you*" or "*Thanks Daddy for taking me out or buying me this treat.*" Likewise you can praise God for the victory many times a day. That's good manners.

But people tend to do just the opposite: people ask God for the same thing over and over, yet they rarely, if ever, thank God and consider it *done*. This kind of "spiritual complaining" will not get results.

REPENT NOW FOR COMPLAINING

Lord, I'm sorry for misunderstanding You and accusing You about

_____

_____

_____

prayer

There are prayers in this book you can pray over and over:

- *Apostles' Creed* — Excellent to confess with your children.
- *Difficult People* (or the Ephesian Prayers) — These are anointed prayers you can pray for any believer any time, especially when you want their eyes to be opened. When people say, "All you can do is pray," I think of the Ephesian Prayers right away!
- *Leaders' Prayer* — When you pray for the success of others, you can usually pray over and over. There are many moving parts and changing circumstances in a leader's life. New challenges. New enemies. Leaders always need our prayers.
- *Morning Praise* — suitable for every morning.

- *Nation* — the Bible instructs us to first pray for our nation before praying for ourselves. We can pray for our nation over and over. Because old people are dying and new people are being born, you could never finish praying for your nation.
- *Pastors* — We should pray for our pastor and mentors daily.
- *Praise* — The best thing to do while you're waiting for an answer to manifest in the natural realm is to praise and worship God. We tend to be long on petitions and short on praise. Reverse that!
- *Warfare Prayer* — This is a declaration of who I am in Christ; my agreement with how God sees me. It's more about changing me and my perspective than about asking God to change a circumstance.
- *Worship* — similar to *Praise*. I will explain the difference in another booklet. It's a topic for worship leaders.

2
BASICS OF PRAYER

> **ISAIAH 43:26** (KJV) Put me in remembrance: let us plead together: declare thou, that thou mayest be justified.

God invites us to "plead" with Him. What does "plead" mean? To plead is to "state your case" or "set forth your evidence." The picture is one of a courtroom. In court, the best case wins. So build a case for yourself before you come to Heaven's throne!

The more Scriptures and Scriptural reasons you have for what you want, the better the case you present before God. God not only wants you to agree with Him, but He also wants to agree with you! You've got to give Him something to agree with. Plead with Him, state your case, give Him your reasons, and present to Him your Scriptures!

People intuitively know how to build a good case in life. My 2-year old told her mother, "Can I have baby app? You set an alarm (for 10 minutes of screen time max). When it dings dings, I give you back. I will not get angry, OK?" That's a 2-year old pleading her case why we should let her have her mother's phone. She knows we want her to have self-control, so she doesn't merely yell and scream, "I want it! I want it!" She thinks about what we want. She knows we want her to learn manners and responsibility, not spend too much screen time and not get angry when an object is taken away. She limited herself and promised to do so with a good attitude.

That's pretty convincing, isn't it? As a parent, you'd want to agree with your child who presents her case well.

When it comes to talking with God, people seem to forget this childlike strategy. They sound doubtful and unsure. They are like people who get nervous talking to someone powerful whom they don't know well.

Let's say you are seeking a new job. How would you persuade your future boss to give you this job? You'd build your case! You'd demonstrate to him or her: Why are you valuable? What can you do for the company? How will you grow the business and make it more profitable?

Generally it's not enough to say, "I'm a good learner" or "I have a degree." The boss is interested to know: What problems have you solved? Can you work in teams? Are you accountable? Do you know how to train others? If you build a good case with compelling reasons and supporting evidence, you will more likely get the job than the unsure seeker!

It's no different when it comes to effective prayer: Build a good case for what you want with good reasons and supporting evidence—that is, with Scriptures. Don't merely say, "I base all my prayers on one verse—Matthew 7:7, 'Ask and you shall receive'."

It is generally not a strong or sufficient case. Do you realize the devil is also pleading against you? Remember the devil is the "false accuser of the brethren" (Revelation 12:10). He's trying to pile up evidence on his side. God wants to agree with you, not the adversary, so our Father invites you to "plead" your case with Him.

LEARNING BY EXAMPLE

To help you learn how to plead your case, I will give you a look into my prayer life. I have included over 60 prayers that have worked for me. They are prayers that got answered.

You can pray them exactly as they are or adjust and amend them to suit your needs. Use them as models for your own prayer life. If you mix your own faith with these Scriptures, you will find the Word works every time!

God said in Jeremiah 1:12 (ASV), "…I watch over my word to perform it." Once you learn how to plead your case, you will be adept at highlighting your own Scriptures, building your own case with God, and getting your own answers for anything you need!

YOUR SUPERNATURAL HELPER

What if you don't know all the Scriptures you need for a specific situation? The Holy Spirit is here to help the born again believer. Romans 8:26 (NET) says, "The Spirit helps us in our weakness, for we do not know how we should pray, but the Spirit himself intercedes for us with inexpressible groaning." You can pray the perfect will of God by praying in other tongues (Romans 8:27-28).

I switch between praying in English and praying in heavenly languages as per Acts 2, 8, 9, 10, and 19. Four times after the Day of Pentecost, the Bible states or implies believers received the gift of praying in tongues. According to Mark 16:17, it is a continuing experience that enriches the life of the believer.

Paul put it this way, *"What is the conclusion then? I will pray with the spirit, and I will also pray with the understanding. I will sing with the spirit, and I will also sing with the understanding."* (1 Corinthians 14:15) Praying in English is praying with my understanding; praying in the spirit is praying in tongues, which is beyond my understanding.

Most people have a preference to pray in the spirit OR pray with their understanding; thus they limit the scope of their own prayer life. God wants both your spirit AND your mind to be engaged in prayer.

*Pleading your case is part of the "prayer of faith" or the prayer to change things and improve circumstances in your life. This is only one of the ways to pray. There are at least 9 types of prayers found in the Bible. To learn more about these, visit us online for the audio series "**9 Types of Prayer.**"*

REPENT FOR ANGER OR BITTERNESS DUE TO PAST FAILURES IN PRAYER.

_____

_____

I believe things are going to be different from now on.

3
PEOPLE I PRAY FOR

> **2 TIMOTHY 2:1-4** (KJV)
>
> **1** I exhort therefore FIRST OF ALL that supplications, prayers, intercessions, *and* giving of thanks be made for all men, **2** for KINGS and all who are in AUTHORITY, that we may lead a quiet and peaceable life in all godliness and reverence. **3** For this *is* good and acceptable in the sight of God our Savior, **4** who desires all men to be saved and to come to the knowledge of the truth.

First things first. God wants us to pray for leaders, and I have always considered spiritual leaders more important than political leaders. So I make a list of people I pray for. "First of all" I am to pray for leaders. Then I pray for my needs.

People often fail in prayer for simple reasons like this… they put things out of order. There is a spiritual order God respects. "First of all" means God expects us to pray for every influencer, because they affect so many other lives, and they are likely facing decisions and temptations only leaders face.

PEOPLE I PRAY FOR

SPIRITUAL LEADERS I LOOK UP TO & PRAY FOR:

1. My Pastor: _____

2. My Mentor: _____

3. My Teacher: _____

4. _____

5. _____

6. _____

7. _____

8. _____

9. _____

Galatians 6:6 says I should not only pray for, but also give to my mentors and teachers. Faith and works go hand in hand.

WORLD LEADERS I PRAY FOR:

1. U.S. President: _____

2. Governor: _____

3. Prime Minister of Israel: _____

4. Prime Minister of _____

5. Premier of _____

6. King of _____

7. _____

8. _____

9. _____

10. _____

EPHESIANS 1:15-16 Therefore I also, AFTER I heard of your FAITH in the Lord Jesus and your LOVE for all the saints, **16** do not cease to give thanks for you, making mention of you in my prayers…

GET PRAYERS ANSWERED

We have a tendency to "pray down" more than "**pray up.**" We tend to pray for people when they're not doing so well, or for people whom we think are worse off than us. Conversely, we tend to relax our prayers for people when they get better. We don't think of praying for people who seem better off than us. Did you know Paul tells us to do the *opposite*?

Paul prayed for his disciples more AFTER he heard of their strong faith and love. Why? Likely because they become a target for the devil. The enemy wants more than anything for successful people to fall. It causes more damage.

Paul prayed his most famous and most powerful prayer—**Ephesians 1:17-23**—for people he thought were doing well!

CELEBRITIES, INFLUENCERS, SUCCESSFUL LEADERS

I ADMIRE OR WANT TO CONNECT WITH:

1. _____
2. _____
3. _____
4. _____
5. _____
6. _____
7. _____
8. _____
9. _____

MY FAMILY:

1. _____
2. _____
3. _____
4. _____
5. _____

PEOPLE I PRAY FOR

6. _____
7. _____
8. _____
9. _____
10. _____

MY CHURCH MEMBERS:

1. _____
2. _____
3. _____
4. _____
5. _____
6. _____
7. _____
8. _____
9. _____
10. _____

MY DISCIPLES:

1. _____
2. _____
3. _____
4. _____
5. _____
6. _____

GET PRAYERS ANSWERED

7. _____

8. _____

9. _____

10. _____

MY CO-WORKERS/ BOSS/ EMPLOYEES:

1. _____

2. _____

3. _____

4. _____

5. _____

6. _____

7. _____

8. _____

9. _____

10. _____

MY FRIENDS/ ACQUAINTANCES:

11. _____

2. _____

3. _____

4. _____

5. _____

6. _____

7. _____

PEOPLE I PRAY FOR

8. _____
9. _____
10. _____

MY NEIGHBORS:

1. _____
2. _____
3. _____
4. _____
5. _____
6. _____
7. _____
8. _____
9. _____
10. _____

SPORTS COACH/ SPORTS BUDDIES/ HOBBY PARTNERS:

1. _____
2. _____
3. _____
4. _____
5. _____
6. _____
7. _____
8. _____

GET PRAYERS ANSWERED

9. _____

10. _____

SINNERS & SEEKERS FOR WHOM I PRAY TO BE SAVED:

1. _____
2. _____
3. _____
4. _____
5. _____
6. _____
7. _____
8. _____
9. _____
10. _____

IMPORTANT PEOPLE TO ME

_____
_____
_____
_____
_____
_____
_____
_____
_____

4
6 STEPS TO SAVE YOUR FAMILY

One of the most common prayer requests I receive wherever I preach is a parent asking for their child to be saved, or a child asking for their parents to be saved. I prayed ONCE for my unsaved loved ones and within a year, nearly everybody in my immediate family was saved.

When someone asks me to pray for their unsaved loved ones, I normally ask, "Have you ever bound Satan from blinding their eyes?" I can safely say 90% of the time, the response is a blank look and a hesitant, "No, am I supposed to?"

This is such an important prayer request. I want you to take the time to digest the following Scriptures *before* praying any more about your family. I also challenge you to stop saying your family member is "stubborn, set in their ways, or hard-headed." Your words have more power than you realize. If you want them saved, stop seeing them the way they are or used to be. Once you read and fully understand what is written below, pray with confidence *once and for all*. I believe you will see a change, just as I have. I declare over you that "as for you AND your house, you will all serve the Lord!" (Joshua 24:15)

1 JOHN 5:14-15 (KJV) And this is the confidence that we have in him, that, if we ask any thing according to his will, he heareth us: **15** And if we know that he hear us, whatsoever we ask, we know that we have the petitions that we desired of him.

Know first that God's Word is God's will. God's Word tells us...

2 PETER 3:9 (KJV) The Lord is not slack concerning his promise, as some men count slackness; but is longsuffering to us-ward, not willing that any should perish, but that all should come to repentance. God wants everyone to be saved!

1 TIMOTHY 2:4 (KJV) Who will have all men to be saved, and to come unto the knowledge of the truth. When we pray according to God's Word, we can pray according to God's Will!

Know secondly the unsaved are victims of satan...satan is blinding their eyes.

1 CORINTHIANS 2:14 (KJV) But the natural man receiveth not the things of the Spirit of God: for they are foolishness unto him: neither can he know them, because they are spiritually discerned.

2 CORINTHIANS 4:3-4 (KJV) But if our gospel be hid, it is hid to them that are lost: **4** In whom the god of this world hath blinded the minds of them which believe not, lest the light of the glorious gospel of Christ, who is the image of God, should shine unto them.

2 CORINTHIANS 10:3-5 (KJV) For though we walk in the flesh, we do not war after the flesh: **4** (For the weapons of our warfare are not carnal, but mighty through God to the pulling down of **strongholds**;) **5** Casting down **imaginations**, and every high thing that exalteth itself against the **knowledge** of God, and bringing into captivity every **thought** to the obedience of Christ;

The "strongholds" set up against the unsaved are called "imaginations" (the margin of a good reference Bible says, "reasonings"), "high thing" (knowledge) and "thought." The Word of God, authoritative prayer and words spoken in love can bring down these strongholds.

STEP 1: Bind the spirits that bind the truth—loose the spirit of the unsaved.

LUKE 10:19 Behold, I give you power to tread on serpents and scorpions and over all the power of the enemy: and nothing shall by any means hurt you.

MATTHEW 18:18-19 (KJV) Verily I say unto you, Whatsoever you shall bind on earth shall be bound in heaven: **19** and whatsoever ye shall loose on earth shall be loosed in heaven.

Say once and for all, "Satan, get your hands off my (name your unsaved loved one)! I break your power over _____'s life in Jesus' Name! I claim _____'s full deliverance and salvation! They belong to God!"

STEP 2: Pray for ears to hear and eyes to see spiritual truth

MATTHEW 13:14-16 (KJV) And in them is fulfilled the prophecy of Esaias, which saith, By hearing ye shall hear, and shall not understand; and seeing ye shall see, and shall not perceive: **15** For this people's heart is waxed gross, and their ears are dull of hearing, and their eyes they have closed; lest at any time they should see with their eyes, and hear with their ears, and should understand with their heart, and should be converted, and I should heal them. **16** But blessed are your eyes, for they see: and your ears, for they hear.

Say, "I pray for _____'s eyes to see and for _____'s ear to be open to the truth."

STEP 3: Pray for their heart to be good ground (soft & ready) to the Truth of the Gospel.

LUKE 8:15 (KJV) But that on the good ground are they, which in an honest and good heart, having heard the word, keep it, and bring forth fruit with patience.

Say, "I pray for _____'s heart to be soft and ready ground for the Gospel. I pray that _____ has an honest and good heart, and when (he/she) hears the Word of God, (he/she) will also be a doer of it and patiently study it and put it to practice."

STEP 4: Pray that the Lord of the Harvest sends laborers across their path

MATTHEW 9:37 (KJV) Then saith he unto his disciples, The harvest truly is plenteous, but the labourers are few; Pray ye therefore the Lord of the harvest, that he will send forth labourers into his harvest.

If you have not already discovered, you will soon find most people close to you (especially your own family) do not want to listen to you. They are not about to admit that you know something they don't! Do not worry. God has other laborers who are more "neutral" than you. Pray that God sends them out to your family and/or friends.

Say, "Lord, You said in Your Word to ask the Father to send laborers into the harvest. I am asking the Father in Jesus' Name to send laborers across _____'s path. May the laborers be honest, full of wisdom and full of the Holy Ghost. Surround _____ with the Gospel for the next 30 days (or longer), so they will see how much You love them!"

STEP 5: Give thanks to God for the answer!

PHILIPPIANS 4:6 (BRG) Be careful for nothing (don't fret, worry or have any anxiety about anything); but in every thing by prayer and supplication with thanksgiving let your requests be made known unto God.

It's easy to thank God after you've seen the answer. But it takes faith to thank God before you see the answer! **Hebrews 11:6** says, "Without faith it is impossible to please God." Thank God by faith! Any time you think of your loved ones from now on, do not pray for them to be saved again, just thank God He's heard and answered your prayer!

STEP 6: Be ready to lead someone to the Lord!

Be ready to share Jesus with someone who is interested. You may be the laborer someone is praying for God to send out! Tell the person that God's requirements are that everyone repent and believe in His Son's sacrifice for them. You must repent not merely from a few sins, while holding on to others, but you must repent of all your sins. Then you turn to God for help by: 1) believing in your heart that Jesus is God, and 2) saying with your mouth that Jesus died and rose again for you!

ROMANS 10:9-10 That if thou shalt confess with thy mouth the Lord Jesus (that Jesus is the Lord), and shalt believe in thine heart that God hath raised him from the dead, thou shalt be saved. **10** For with the heart man believeth unto righteousness; and with the mouth confession is made unto salvation.

Sample prayer: *"Dear God, please forgive me for all my sins. I repent and turn to Jesus. Today I believe You died on the Cross to take away my sins, and after 3 days You rose again from the dead to give me new life. You are the sinless Son of God. I call Jesus' my Savior and Lord. I am now a born again child of God! Thank You Father for accepting me, in Jesus' Name! Amen."*

5
AGING

ISAIAH 46:4 Even to your old age, I am He, and even to gray hairs I will carry you! I have made, and I will bear; Even I will carry, and will deliver you.

CONFESS: *God is good and faithful to the end. He will carry me and deliver me. This is a divine promise.*

PSALM 37:25-26 I have been young, and now am old; Yet I have not seen the righteous forsaken, Nor his descendants begging bread. **26** He is ever merciful, and lends; And his descendants are blessed.

CONFESS: *I'm rich till old age. I have more than enough to lend and give to my children and grandchildren.*

DEUTERONOMY 34:7 And Moses was an hundred and twenty years old when he died: his **eye** was not dim, nor his **natural force** abated.

CONFESS: *Moses could walk and see on his own at 120. You renewed his youth like the eagle's (Psalm 103:5). I confess the same strength lives in me. Dear Lord, do remind me that Moses' biggest mistake came later in life when he got angry and lost his temper. I will not misuse my maturity as a license to not listen to others, to be insistent, or to get grumpy and demanding, in Jesus' Name. I guard my heart with all diligence, for out of it are the issues of life (Proverbs 4:23).*

PROVERBS 20:29-30 The glory of young men is their strength, And the splendor of old men is their gray head. **30** Blows that hurt cleanse away evil, As do stripes the inner depths of the heart.

CONFESS: *Getting gray hair is a sign of glory. God is glorified in my getting older and wiser. I am not to stop growing. If I become stubborn in my old age, blows that hurt will cleanse away my evil, and stripes will purify the inner depths of my heart. Lord, keep me from being stiff, stuck and stagnant. Give me a freshness of spirit, a vitality of health and let me glorify you more as I age more.*

HAGGAI 2:9 (KJV) The glory of this latter house shall be greater than of the former, saith the Lord of hosts: and in this place will I give peace, saith the Lord of hosts.

CONFESS: *The glory of my latter house [family, ministry] shall be greater than of the former. In Christ, things get better and better. The best is yet to come!*

ECCLESIASTES 7:8-10 The end of a thing is better than its beginning; The patient in spirit is better than the proud in spirit. **9** Do not hasten in your spirit to be angry, For anger rests in the bosom of fools. 10 Do not say, "Why were the former days better than these?" For you do not inquire wisely concerning this.

CONFESS: *The end of something is meant to be better than the beginning. My end will be better than my beginning. The glory of my latter house/ church/ business shall be greater than the glory of the former. I remember not the former things, nor consider the things of old. The "good old days" were not so good. My future is brighter than my past. I remain patient in my old age. I will not rush to be angry. My days are filled with God's peace. Better to be patient than to become proud and fall in the end.*

JOEL 2:28 And it shall come to pass afterward That I will pour out My Spirit on all flesh; Your sons and your daughters shall prophesy, Your old men shall dream dreams, Your young men shall see visions.

NOTE: In the Old Testament, old men came first and led the supernatural revival. This order is reversed when Peter quotes Joel: "Your young men shall see visions, Your old men shall dream dreams." (Acts 2:17)

CONFESS: *The Holy Spirit is being poured out on my flesh. I am open to receiving dreams and visions from the Lord. I am yielded to You, Holy Spirit. Let Your spiritual gifts flow through me. Give me supernatural eyes to see, and supernatural ears to hear. Old men shall dream dreams; young men shall see visions. I will lead and be part of the last days revival.*

2 PETER 3:18 But grow in grace, and in the knowledge of our Lord and Saviour Jesus Christ. To him be glory both now and forever. Amen.

CONFESS: *Dear Lord, help me grow in grace.*

ISAIAH 43:18-19 "Do not remember the former things, Nor consider the things of old. **19** Behold, I will do a new thing, Now it shall spring forth; Shall you not know it? I will even make a road in the wilderness.

REVELATION 21:4 And God will wipe away every tear from their eyes; there shall be no more death, nor sorrow, nor crying. There shall be no more pain, for the former things have passed away."

A related chapter you can skip to is "Healing."

6
ANCIENT PRAYERS

These are the most ancient prayers that get answered. The first is known as the "**Aaronic Blessing**," which Aaron, the first high priest, and subsequent high priests prayed over the people of Israel. No wonder Jews are disproportionately blessed everywhere they live!

NUMBERS 6:23-27

23 "Speak to Aaron and his sons, saying, 'This is the way you shall bless the children of Israel. Say to them:

24 "The Lord bless you and keep you;

25 The Lord make His face shine upon you, And be gracious to you;

26 The Lord lift up His countenance upon you, And give you peace.' "

Today, through the Atonement of Yeshua the Messiah (Jesus Christ), these blessings belong to us!

Below is a list of blessings that are yours because Jesus has fulfilled all the commandments of the Law for us. Without Jesus we are lawbreakers, deserving only the curse. But with Jesus, we become righteous by grace through faith, and the blessings of the righteous fall on us. Count these blessings (I've put them in all caps)! Confess these blessings!

LEVITICUS 26:3-12 (KJV)

3 If ye walk in my statutes, and keep my commandments, and do them; **4** Then I will give you RAIN in due season, and the land shall yield her INCREASE, and the trees of the field shall yield their FRUIT...

6 And I will give PEACE in the land, and ye shall lie down, and none shall make you afraid: and I will RID EVIL BEASTS out of the land, neither shall the SWORD go through your land.

7 And ye shall chase your ENEMIES, and they shall FALL before you by the sword.

8 And five of you shall CHASE a hundred, and a hundred of you shall put ten thousand to flight: and your ENEMIES shall FALL before you by the sword.

9 For I will have RESPECT unto you, and make you FRUITFUL, and MULTIPLY you, and ESTABLISH my covenant with you.

10 And ye shall EAT old store, and bring forth the OLD because of the NEW.

11 And I will SET MY TABERNACLE among you: and my soul shall not abhor you.

12 And I will WALK among you, and will BE YOUR GOD, and ye shall BE MY PEOPLE.

The Aaronic Blessing of Numbers 6 is the basis for the blessing Jewish parents speak over their children each Sabbath (see the chapter on "Sabbath Blessing").

7
APOSTLES' CREED

Apostles' Creed. The Apostles' Creed represents the core beliefs of Christianity on which the first Apostles agreed ["credo" means "I believe" in Latin]. I say this with my family.

1. I believe in God the Father, Almighty, Creator of Heaven and earth.
2. I believe in Jesus Christ, His only Son, our Lord.
3. He was conceived by the power of the Holy Spirit, born of the Virgin Mary
4. Under Pontius Pilate, He was crucified, died, and was buried.
5. He descended to the dead. On the third day He rose again.
6. He ascended into Heaven and is seated at the right hand of the Father.
7. He will come again to judge the living and the dead.
8. I believe in the Holy Spirit,
9. the holy Christian Church, the communion of saints,
10. the forgiveness of sins,
11. the resurrection of the body,
12. and the life everlasting. Amen.

APOSTLES' CREED

prayer

There is an expanded version of this **Christian statement of faith** adopted at the **First Council of Nicea** in 325AD. It was amended slightly at the **First Council at Constantinople** (present day Istanbul, Turkey) in 381AD. Most notably the second and present version clarified the Divinity of the Holy Spirit.

The Nicene Creed is the only creed agreed upon by all three main branches of Christianity: Western Catholic, Eastern Orthodox and Protestant. When you hear anti-Christian mockers ridicule the Bible and claim that its message is so subjective that it can be interpreted in any way, and Christians don't agree on anything, you can tell them it's not true. The Apostles' Creed and subsequent Nicene Creed documented for nearly 2000 years the 12 major doctrines all true Christians agree upon! Make a habit of confessing it.

THE NICENE CREED

1. We believe in one God, the Father Almighty, Maker of heaven and earth, and of all things visible and invisible;

2. and in one Lord Jesus Christ, the only-begotten Son of God, begotten of the Father before all worlds; God of God, Light of Light, very God of very God; begotten, not made, being of one substance with the Father, by whom all things were made.

3. Who, for us men for our salvation, came down from heaven, and was incarnate by the Holy Spirit of the virgin Mary, and was made man;

4. and was crucified also for us under Pontius Pilate;

5. He suffered and was buried; and the third day He rose again, according to the Scriptures;

6. and ascended into heaven, and sits on the right hand of the Father;

7. He shall come again, with glory, to judge the quick and the dead; whose kingdom shall have no end.

8. We believe in the Holy Ghost, the Lord and Giver of Life; who proceeds

from the Father and the Son; who with the Father and the Son together is worshipped and glorified; who spoke by the prophets.

9. We believe in one, holy, Christian and apostolic Church.

10. We acknowledge one baptism for the remission of sins; and

11. we look for the resurrection of the dead,

12. and the life of the world to come. Amen.

The Nicene Creed re-written by a child—
Jessica Azzolini when she was 9-years old

I believe in God the Father who created the world. He made everything that you can see and everything you can't. I believe that God had a Son called Jesus who He sent to teach us many things on Earth. He was God on Earth. God is all powerful and all knowing. Jesus' mother was Mary. She got a visit from an angel filled with the Holy Spirit and was made pregnant. He came down from Heaven. He performed many miracles and made the sick people better. After many years He died on a cross and was buried for our sake but then He came back to life. He went back up to Heaven and is seated at God's right hand. There is always a place for Him in Heaven and in Earth. I believe that He will come again and that He will never die. I believe in the Holy Spirit, another piece of God. Along with God and Jesus, people love and praise the Holy Spirit, and the wisest men even talk about the Holy Spirit. I believe in one church. I say that I have been baptized for forgiveness of my mistakes and I look forward to when Jesus will come back. Amen.

8
ASSASSINATION

No one can deny the miracle of President **Donald Trump**'s surviving the assassination attempt on July 13, 2024 and again on September 15, 2024. I remember the moment I heard of the first failed attempt, I thanked God that He heard our prayers. From exactly 3 years and 9 months —1369 days—we prayed for his protection. These prayers got answered.

You may never face an assassination attempt, but you may have to deal with serious harassment, defamation or character assassination. Don't be discouraged. Don't give up! Learn these Scriptures for serious protection.

PSALM 23:4 Even though I walk through the valley of the shadow of death, I will fear no evil, for You are with me; Your rod and Your staff, they comfort me.

PSALM 27:1 The Lord is my light and my salvation; Whom shall I fear? The Lord is the strength of my life; Of whom shall I be afraid?

PRAY: *Thank You, Father, for making Donald Trump fearless [replace with the name of a current leader under threat—RFK, Jr., Alex Jones, Elon Musk, etc.]*

ISAIAH 41:10 Fear not, for I am with you; be not dismayed, for I am your God; I will strengthen you, I will help you, I will uphold you with My righteous right hand.

GET PRAYERS ANSWERED

prayer

PSALM 121:5-8 The Lord is your keeper; The Lord is your shade at your right hand. The sun shall not strike you by day, Nor the moon by night [nor a bullet any time]. The Lord shall preserve you from all evil [assassinations]; He shall preserve your soul. The Lord shall preserve your going out [to rallies, courts or prison] and your coming in [to your home or the White House] From this time forth, and even forevermore.

ISAIAH 54:17 No weapon formed against you shall prosper, And every tongue which rises against you in judgment You shall condemn. This is the heritage of the servants of the Lord, And their righteousness is from Me," Says the Lord.

PSALM 91:4 He shall cover you with His feathers, And under His wings you shall take refuge; His truth shall be your shield and buckler.

PRAY: *Your truth is our shield and buckler [body armor or wall]. Under Your wings we take refuge. No one can harass us or attack us successfully. Thank You for protecting us from time wasters and trouble makers, in Jesus' Name.*

ZECHARIAH 2:5 For I, says the Lord, will be a wall of fire all around her, and I will be the glory in her midst.

PRAY: *You are the Wall of Fire around our house and our family. You are the Wall of Fire around Donald Trump.*

PSALM 10:15 Break the arm of the wicked and the evil man; Seek out his wickedness until You find none."

PSALM 125:2 As the mountains surround Jerusalem, So the Lord surrounds His people From this time forth and forever.

LUKE 10:19 Behold, I give you the authority to trample on serpents and scorpions, and over all the power of the enemy, and nothing shall by any means hurt you.

PRAY: *No weapon, no bullet, no poison can hurt us. We have authority and we trample over the enemy.*

ASSASSINATION

prayer

BOOMERANG PRAYER

ESTHER 7:10 So they hanged Haman on the gallows that he had prepared for Mordecai. Then the king's wrath subsided.

PSALM 7:15-16 He made a pit and dug it out, And has fallen into the ditch which he made. His trouble shall return upon his own head, And his violent dealing shall come down on his own crown."

PRAY: *Let evil return, Father, on its own head.*

PROVERBS 26:27 Whoever digs a pit will fall into it, And he who rolls a stone will have it roll back on him."

PRAY: *Roll the stone back on the evil doers. Let their weapons backfire. Let their knives cut themselves, but not the innocent. Let them fall into their own traps. We will see the curse reverse on the curser and give glory to God for being our shield.*

PSALM 9:15 The nations have sunk down in the pit which they made; In the net which they hid, their own foot is caught."

PRAY: *We pray against international conspiracies, wrong foreign policies and provocative national security decisions. May foreign actors get caught in their own net, and may the Deep State fall into the pit they dug for me.*

The best Psalm for praying that a curse boomerang back to the sender is Psalm 35. It explains in verse 7 that their plot to hurt must be morally unjust or "without cause." It doesn't matter if their scheme is "legal". God will work against law fare or the weaponization of law against an innocent person.

GET PRAYERS ANSWERED

prayer

PSALM 35:1-8

1 Plead my cause, O Lord, with those who strive with me; **Fight against those who fight against me**.

2 Take hold of shield and buckler, And stand up for my help.

3 Also draw out the spear, And **stop those who pursue me**. Say to my soul, "**I am your salvation**." [The Lord will reveal His Salvation or Yeshua His Son to the persecuted one.]

4 Let those be put to shame and brought to dishonor Who seek after my life; Let those be turned back and brought to confusion Who plot my hurt.

5 Let them be like chaff before the wind, And **let the angel of the Lord chase them**.

6 Let their way be dark and slippery, And **let the angel of the Lord pursue them**.

7 For **without cause** they have hidden their net for me in a pit, Which they have dug without cause for my life.

8 Let destruction come upon him unexpectedly [KJV unawares, NET by surprise], And **let his net that he has hidden catch himself**; Into that very destruction let him fall.

9
AVENGE ME

Jesus taught us how to pray for justice. Why don't we do it?

LUKE 18:1-8

1 Then He spoke a parable to them, that men always ought to pray and not lose heart,

2 saying: "There was in a certain city a judge who did not fear God nor regard man.

3 Now there was a widow in that city; and she came to him, saying, '**Get justice** for me from my adversary.'

4 And he would not for a while; but afterward he said within himself, 'Though I do not fear God nor regard man,

5 yet because this widow troubles me I will **avenge her**, lest by her continual coming she weary me.'"

6 Then the Lord said, "Hear what the unjust judge said.

7 And shall God not **avenge His own elect** who cry out day and night to Him, though He bears long with them?

8 I tell you that He will **avenge them speedily**. Nevertheless, when the Son of Man comes, will He really find faith on the earth?"

When is it OK to pray for justice like this woman did? When is it OK to pray, *"Lord, avenge me"*?

3 PRINCIPLES *Before* PRAYING FOR JUSTICE

1. The first principle to follow before praying for justice is that we must not be unjust ourselves.

Jesus asked, "Why do you see the speck in your brother's eye, but fail to see the beam of wood in your own? Or how can you say to your brother, 'Let me remove the speck from your eye,' while there is a beam in your own? You hypocrite! First remove the beam from your own eye, and then you can see clearly to remove the speck from your brother's eye." (Matthews 7:3-5 NET)

We are to remove the log out of our own eyes before we go about removing the speck out of other people's eyes. Christians have wrongly assumed Jesus meant we are not to notice something stuck in another person's eye. Of course, we will notice and we can help others. But first, we must make sure we're not guilty ourselves.

2. The second principle is that we need to extend grace and mercy to our enemies before judging them.

The hope is that they will repent, stop their sinning and reconcile. This is the normal way wars are conducted: terms of peace are sent first; if they get rejected, then war begins. To start a war without offering conditions of peace is unjust. This is why Jesus emphasized loving your enemies to the first-century Jews. They judged others, especially Gentiles, before taking this step.

"Love your enemies, do good to those who hate you, bless those who curse you, pray for those who mistreat you. To the person who strikes you on the cheek, offer the other as well, and from the person who takes away your coat, do not withhold your tunic either…" (Luke 6:27-31 NET)

3. The third principle is to stop giving grace and mercy to hardened criminals and unrepentant sinners, and sue for justice.

When our enemies refuse to make peace, it would be foolish to keep trying to reconcile and extend the olive branch of peace while they are actively trying to destroy you or harm other innocent people. When Palestinians were given land for peace, they continued to attack Jewish civilians (such as in the surprise War of October 7, 2023). Christians don't know how to respond. They are confused. They are stuck at "love your enemies." Israel had already extended the olive branch of peace, but in return they had their citizens murdered, kidnapped, raped and tortured. Does the Bible tell believers to give grace to terrorists?

No. Extending mercy to repeat criminals and allowing injustice to prolong is itself an *injustice*. It makes you an accomplice to the crime you could have prevented. Accomplices deserve the same punishment as the main actors.

I do not want to be an accessory to crime! God does not call me to make peace with evil. That's not Biblical. At some point, either the enemy changes or we must change. We are to use a different tool in the Bible to bring about justice, without ever seeking revenge or taking vengeance into our own hands.

THE 4-STEP PROCESS OF DEALING WITH SINNERS

Jesus explained the 4-step process in Matthew 18, "If your brother sins, (step 1) go and show him his fault when you two are alone. If he listens to you, you have regained your brother. But if he does not listen, (step 2) take one or two others with you, so that at the testimony of two or three witness every matter may be established. If he refuses to listen to them, (step 3) tell it to the church. If he refuses to listen to the church, (step 4) treat him like a Gentile or a tax collector. (How?) I tell you the truth, whatever you bind on earth will have been bound in heaven, and whatever you relate on earth will have been released in heaven." (Matthew 18:15-18 NET)

The context of this "binding and losing" Scripture is not dealing with devils, but dealing with human injustice! It's a conflict resolution protocol. When there's conflict and your enemy refuses to reconcile, but rather persists in doing harm to you or others, you have the power and authority to "bind" such an unjust character.

The Apostle Paul did it to the man who had sex with his father's new wife. Paul didn't tell the Christians, "All you can do is love him and give him more grace." No! He said, "Turn this man over to Satan for the destruction of the flesh, so that his spirit may be saved in the day of the Lord." (1 Corinthians 5:5 NET)

Paul was very loving to "bind" him and "turn him over to Satan." Justice made this man repent. Without divine judgment, this man could have been lost eternally.

I'm convinced Jesus gave the spiritually mature Church much more power than we realize or use. The immature Church should be trained to walk in love and forgiveness first. But the mature Church should be **carriers of justice**.

Jesus said this at the end of discipling twelve men for three and a half years, and after His death, burial and resurrection, "If you forgive anyone's sins, they are forgiven; if you retain anyone's sins, they are retained." (John 20:23) What an amazing statement! Do we teach or practice this? If they could learn this in three and a half years, how about us? Jesus wants to trust us, after we've been trained properly! This power He confers on us trained disciples is called **judicial power.** We who have been spiritually developed have the **power to acquit or convict**.

This power must be handled humbly, gently, carefully—in other words, Scripturally. We are not to go around judging people. We are not to go cursing everyone who wrong us. But when facing a difficult situation (like a relentless harasser, unrepentant attacker, or irreconcilable bad actor), we have the right to retain their sin and cry out to the Lord, *"Avenge me! Get justice for me from my adversary!"*

prayer

PSALM 143:9-12 Deliver me from my enemies, O Lord! I have fled to you for refuge. **10** Teach me to do your will, for you are my God! Let your good Spirit lead me on level ground! **11** For your name's sake, O Lord, preserve my life! In your righteousness bring my soul out of trouble! **12** And in your steadfast love you will CUT OFF my enemies, and you will DESTROY all the adversaries of my soul, for I am your servant.

PSALM 37:6 (NKJ) He shall bring forth your righteousness as the **light**, And your justice as the **noonday**.

(NLT) He will make your innocence radiate like the **dawn**, and the justice of your cause will shine like the noonday **sun**.

(NIV) He will make your righteous reward shine like the **dawn**, your vindication like the noonday **sun**.

NOT AGAIN!

Closely related to "avenge me" is "not again!" If you want to pray for injustice not to repeat, I would use these Scriptures.

ISAIAH 42:3 A bruised reed He will not break, And smoking flax He will not quench; He will bring forth JUSTICE for truth.

MATTHEW 12:20 A bruised reed He will not break, And smoking flax He will not quench, Till He sends forth JUSTICE to victory;

PROVERBS 26:2 Like a flitting sparrow, like a flying swallow, So a curse without cause shall not alight [The King James Version says, "The curse causeless shall not come."]

PRAY (together with your spouse if you're married): *"Lord, You promised in Your Word that You will not allow a curse to come on me twice. A bruised reed You will not break. I have been bruised for my own good. You said, 'The blueness of a wound cleanest away evil: so do stripes the inward parts of the belly' (Proverbs 20:30 KJV). Because of my suffering, I am a better person. I refuse to fear a repeat situation.*

"I commit this situation to you and I declare, 'Not again! Never again!' I've learned my lesson. Forgive me for worrying, holding grudges and taking matters into my own hands in the past. Now I'm a different man/ woman. I choose to put all my trust in Jesus who redeemed me from the curse of the law, being made a curse for me on the Cross of Calvary (Galatians 3:13). I have the Holy Spirit in me. I can walk in love and forgiveness. I refuse to hold a grudge. I shut the door to the enemy.

"Satan, I'm walking in love, so you can't touch me! Stop your lies, accusations, and get out of my (life/ family/ business/ church) in Jesus' Mighty Name!"

10
BOOKS

WHY I WRITE BOOKS

Here are 12 Scriptures that motivate me to obey God's call to write. When I'm discouraged, they remind me "why" I must write books. Without these 12 why's, you would not be holding this book in your hands.

You must find your own why's.

1) LUKE 1:3 It seemed good to me also, having had perfect understanding of all things from the very first, to WRITE to you an orderly account, most excellent Theophilus,

Luke was led by the Spirit to write 2 books—the Gospel of Luke and the Book of Acts. He did it based on a personal leading that was no more spectacular than "it seemed good."

No vision. No angel told him. Just a mere "it seemed good" was enough for Luke to document an orderly account of Jesus' life. How grateful we are that Luke was inspired to write!

2) REVELATION 1:11 "I am the Alpha and the Omega, the First and the Last," and, "What you see, WRITE in a book and SEND it to the seven churches which are in Asia...

3) HABAKKUK 2:2 Then the LORD answered me and said: "WRITE the vision and make it plain on tablets, that he may RUN who reads it.

4) JOHN 20:30-31 30 And truly Jesus did many other signs in the presence of His disciples, which are not written in this book; **31** but these are WRITTEN THAT you may believe that Jesus is the Christ, the Son of God, and THAT believing you may have life in His name.

5) JOHN 21:25 And there are also many other things that Jesus did, which if they were WRITTEN one by one, I suppose that even the world itself could not contain the books that would be written. Amen.

6) JUDE 1:3-4 (NIV) **3** Dear friends, although I was very eager to WRITE to you about the salvation we share, I felt compelled to WRITE and urge you to contend for the faith that was once for all entrusted to God's holy people. **4** For certain men whose condemnation was WRITTEN about long ago have secretly slipped in among you. They are godless men, who change the grace of our God into a licence for immorality and deny Jesus Christ our only Sovereign and Lord.

7) 1 JOHN 1:4 And these things we WRITE to you that your joy may be full.

8) 2 JOHN 1:12 Having many things to WRITE to you, I did not wish to do so with paper and ink; but I hope to come to you and speak face to face, that our joy may be full.

9) EXODUS 17:14 Then the LORD said to Moses, "WRITE this for a memorial in the book and recount it in the hearing of Joshua, that I will utterly blot out the remembrance of Amalek from under heaven."

10) EXODUS 24:12 Then the LORD said to Moses, "Come up to Me on the mountain and be there; and I will give you tablets of stone, and the law and commandments which I have WRITTEN, that you may teach them."

11) JEREMIAH 30:2 "Thus speaks the LORD God of Israel, saying: 'WRITE in a book for yourself all the words that I have spoken to you.

12) JEREMIAH 36:2 Take a scroll of a book and WRITE on it all the words that I have spoken to you against Israel, against Judah, and against all the nations, from the day I spoke to you, from the days of Josiah even to this day.

prayer

GET PRAYERS ANSWERED

Action: I will set a schedule to write and finish my books on these topics or with these proposed titles (including START and END dates):

11
CHILDREN

Praying for God-Sent Children

Tip: Whether you are expecting a child on the way or already have children, these Scriptures are great to pray over your family. I confessed these Scriptures before we had our first daughter, and it is amazing to see how these godly words have produced a godly, pleasant, obedient child. Now I have four uniquely different children who span a broad range of ages. All of them are a pleasure to me.

Some of these Scriptures are about the child, while many are about us as parents.

To pray *for* children, i.e. for a couple to conceive, please go to the chapter "Pregnancy."

Blessings on My Family

GENESIS 18:19 For I have known him, in order that he may command his children and his household after him, that they keep the way of the LORD, to do righteousness and justice, that the LORD may bring to Abraham what He has spoken to him."

COMMENT: God blessed Abraham with the most successful family on earth, mainly because He knew that Abraham would lead his children to

God. Not every man leads. A lot of men abdicate their role and make excuses like, "My wife is in charge of that stuff (raising children)." God said He KNEW Abraham would lead his children to God. That made Abraham irresistible to the Creator.

PRAY: *Father, You know me, that I will command my children and my household after me, that they keep the Way of the Lord (another name for Christianity is "The Way"). I will teach them to do what is right and be an example of justice to them. My main job as a parent is to model God to them, and You are never unjust. I am a representative of God and a model of justice to my children, in Jesus' Name.*

GENESIS 22:18 In your seed all the nations of the earth shall be blessed, because you have obeyed My voice."

GENESIS 26:4 And I will make your descendants multiply as the stars of heaven; I will give to your descendants all these lands; and in your seed all the nations of the earth shall be blessed;

GENESIS 28:14 Also your descendants shall be as the dust of the earth; you shall spread abroad to the west and the east, to the north and the south; and in you and in your seed all the families of the earth shall be blessed.

GALATIAN 3:14 that the blessing of Abraham might come upon the Gentiles in Christ Jesus, that we might receive the promise of the Spirit through faith.

1 SAMUEL 2:26 And the child Samuel grew in stature, and in favor both with the LORD and men.

PRAY: *My children will grow in stature (be physically healthy and well-developed), and grow in favor both with the Lord and men.*

> ### LUKE 1:80, 2:40
>
> 80 So the child grew and became strong in spirit, and was in the deserts till the day of his manifestation to Israel.
>
> 40 And the Child grew and became strong in spirit, filled with wisdom; and the grace of God was upon Him.

PRAY: *Just as Jesus grew, even though He was the Son of God, so too my children grow and become strong in spirit, filled with wisdom, and the grace of God is upon*

CHILDREN

them. I confess that my children grow up to be loyal to God and loyal to us as parents, in Jesus' Name.

ISAIAH 8:18 (KJV) Behold, I and the children whom the LORD hath given me are for signs and for wonders in Israel from the LORD of hosts, which dwelleth in mount Zion.

PRAY: *I and the children whom the Lord has given me, we are for signs and for wonder. When people meet us, they wonder! They ask me how to save their children, their family and themselves. When I appear somewhere, I am a sign convicting people of sin and pointing people to Christ!*

PSALM 37:25-26 (KJV) I have been young, and now am old; yet have I not seen the righteous forsaken, nor his seed begging bread. 26 He is ever merciful, and lendeth; and his seed is blessed.

PRAY: *I have been young, and now I'm middle-aged; yet I have not seen the righteous forsaken, nor my seed begging bread. I am merciful and lend and my seed is blessed. My children will do better than me because they will reap all I have sown and know the valuable of a godly heritage. They will not despise but highly prize their legacy.*

PSALM 112:1-3 1 Praise the LORD! Blessed is the man who fears the LORD, who delights greatly in His commandments. **2** His descendants will be mighty on earth; the generation of the upright will be blessed. **3** Wealth and riches will be in his house, and his righteousness endures forever.

PSALM 127:3 (KJV) Lo, children are an heritage of the LORD: and the fruit of the womb is his reward.

PRAY: *My children are a gift from God. The fruit of my wife's womb is my reward.*

PROVERBS 11:21 (TLB) You can be very sure the evil man will not go unpunished forever. And you can also be very sure God will rescue the children of the godly.

PRAY: *God will rescue my children and keep them away from evil people. Ungodly associations will break up quickly. Any evil person who tries to get near them will swiftly meet with the heavy hand of judgment and be severely punished, in Jesus' Name!*

PROVERBS 13:22 (KJV) A good man leaves an inheritance to his children's children, but the wealth of the sinner is stored up for the righteous.

PRAY: *Make me so wealthy that I leave an inheritance not only for my children, but also my grandchildren. I believe the wealth of the sinner is stored up for me, the righteous. I believe in an end-time transfer of wealth. It's coming to me and my family for the purpose of serving You.*

ACTS 2:39 (KJV) For the promise is to you and to your children, and to all who are afar off, as many as the Lord our God will call."

COMMENT: God treated family members as one unit. When one got saved, all got saved. When one got filled, all got filled with the Holy Spirit and spoke in tongues together.

Western families tend to raise children to be so independent that they grow up without following the faith of their fathers. They leave church and abandon their faith. It's a tragedy.

To give your children good food and good education only to lose them to the devil is foolish. You restrict their choice of food when they're young (they don't know what's best to eat, do they?) and you make them go to school and do their homework. So why would you checkout spiritually when it comes to God and the Bible? Why would you say, "I'll let them decide. I can't force them. They have to make up their own minds"?

You are handing your most precious gifts to the enemy who will diligently train your children in the ways of darkness and hell. Remember Peter's first sermon on Pentecost. He told his unsaved listeners: The promise of God is to "you and your children," not to you alone.

PRAY: *The promise of God is to "me and my children," not to me only. God treats my family members and I as one unit. O Lord, cause my family to be unified in faith and in service to You Lord. If anyone is not, rebuke them sharply and let them kick against the pricks till they run back to You. (Acts 9:5, 26:14) As for me and my house, we will serve the Lord! (Joshua 24:15)*

2 TIMOTHY 3:15 ...that from childhood you have known the Holy Scriptures, which are able to make you wise for salvation through faith which is in Christ Jesus.

ISAIAH 61:7, 9 Instead of your shame you shall have double honor, and instead of confusion they shall rejoice in their portion. Therefore in their land they shall possess double; everlasting joy shall be theirs... **9** Their descendants shall be known among the Gentiles, and their offspring among the people. All who see them shall acknowledge them, that they are the posterity whom the LORD has blessed.

ISAIAH 65:23-24 They shall not labor in vain, nor bring forth children for trouble; for they shall be the descendants of the blessed of the LORD, and their offspring with them. **24** It shall come to pass that before they call, I will answer; and while they are still speaking, I will hear.

Pray: *I will not labor in vain, nor bring forth children for trouble. My children are attentive to God, listen to their parents, and gain wisdom beyond their years. They will make my work worthwhile, and they will be more productive and successful than me. They are descendants of the blessed of the Lord, and even their offsprings are blessed with them. They will have supernatural experiences in prayer that deepen their relationship with the Lord. They will see their prayers answered and they will never leave the Lord.*

Scriptures for Parents' Responsibilities

PROVERBS 22:6 Train up a child in the way he should go, and when he is old he will not depart from it.

PROVERBS 29:15 The rod and rebuke give wisdom, but a child left to himself brings shame to his mother.

DEUTERONOMY 4:9 Only take heed to yourself, and diligently keep yourself, lest you forget the things your eyes have seen, and lest they depart from your heart all the days of your life. And teach them to your children and your grandchildren,

DEUTERONOMY 6:7-9 You shall teach them diligently to your children, and shall talk of them when you sit in your house, when you walk by the way, when you lie down, and when you rise up. **8** You shall bind them as a sign on your hand, and they shall be as frontlets between your eyes. **9** You shall write them on the doorposts of your house and on your gates.

DEUTERONOMY 31:12-13 Gather the people together, men and women and little ones, and the stranger who is within your gates, that they may hear and that they may learn to fear the LORD your God and carefully observe all the words of this law, **13** and that their children, who have not known it, may hear and learn to fear the LORD your God as long as you live in the land which you cross the Jordan to possess."

JEREMIAH 29:5-7 Build houses and dwell in them; plant gardens and eat their fruit. **6** Take wives and beget sons and daughters; and take wives for your sons and give your daughters to husbands, so that they may bear sons and daughters—that you may be increased there, and not diminished. **7** And seek the peace [welfare, prosperity] of the city where I have caused you to be carried away captive, & pray to the LORD for it; for in its peace you will have peace [prosper].

Children I pray for by name with Scriptures

_____

_____

_____

_____

_____

_____

_____

_____

_____

_____

_____

_____

_____

_____

_____

_____

12

CHURCH

Father, in the Name of Jesus, we come into Your presence, giving thanks for _____ [my church name]. You have called us to be a family in God's local church, to be saints in the Body of Christ, to be the salt of _____ [my town or city] and the light of the world. We recognize that You are God, and everything including _____ [my church] was made by You and for You. We use our faith to call into being those things that be not as though they were.

We thank You that we all speak the same thing: there is no division among us; we are perfectly joined together in the same mind and in the same judgment (opinion about spiritual matters, conviction and common purpose, as per 1 Corinthians 1:10). Grant unto us, your representatives, a boldness to speak Your Word which You will confirm with signs following. We thank You that we have workmen in abundance gifted in every manner of workmanship, to design artistic works, to cut jewels, carve wood, and build anything good for God (Exodus 31). All our staff and volunteers are men and women of good reputation, full of the Holy Spirit and wisdom (Acts 6:3). They operate in excellence and are good team players. We have in our church all the ministry gifts for the edifying of the body till we all come into the unity of the faith, and the knowledge of the Son of God, to a perfect man, to the measure of the stature of the fullness of Christ. None of our people act like children, tossed to and fro and carried about with every wind of doctrine, by the trickery of men, in the cunning craftiness of deceitful plotting. But speaking the truth in love, we grow up in all things into Him who is our head, even Christ (Ephesians 4:11-15).

We are a growing are witnessing body of believers becoming bigger and stronger. We have divine favor and grace. We have a good name in the community and the Body of Christ.

Father, we thank You for ministry facilities and websites that will more than meet the needs of the ministry You have called us to. Our church is prospering financially. We have everything we need to carry out Your Great Commission and reach _____ [my nation] for Jesus. We have more than enough to serve You and sow to others.

We are a people of the Word. Jesus is our Lord. The Holy Spirit is our guide. We are teachable, prompt to obey and ready to serve. We are a people of the Spirit; we are willing to testify, prophesy and glorify Jesus at every opportunity. We are a people of love; the love of God is shed abroad in our hearts by the Holy Spirit who's given to us, so we are forgiving and speak the truth in love (Romans 5:5). We are lovers of different cultures, friends of sinners, and soul winners. We are a free people; we have been called to liberty; only we do not use liberty as an opportunity for the flesh, to get our own way, but through love serve one another (Galatians 5:13).

We are a supernatural church, composed of supernatural people doing supernatural things, for we are laborers together with God. We thank You for Your presence among us and we lift holy hands in praise to Your Holy Name! Amen.

More Scripture References: Acts 4:24,29, Exodus 35:33, Romans 4:17, Philippians 4:19, 1 Corinthians 3:19, Mark 16:20, Psalm 63:4.

Ways I can bless my church

_____

_____

_____

_____

13
CHURCH GROWTH

Should our church grow? Every living thing grows. The universe itself is expanding. What do we call a tree that stops growing? *Dead*.

The church is a living organism, therefore it should grow in both depth of discipleship and breadth of disciples—in both quality and quantity of believers. These days, we can grow online and offline.

The walls have come down and the possibilities are limitless. We can talk and pray with anyone around the world virtually any time. People come to Christ and receive healing online. Through Discover Church Online, we are growing 24/7 in prayer, discipleship, worship, serving, video production, book publishing, faith-based travels, and global missions. Growth is the result of God's Word being put to action.

THE PROMISE OF INCREASE

PROVERBS 14:28 (KJV) In the multitude of people is the king's honour; but in the want of people is the destruction of the prince.

COMMENT: A kingdom without people is no kingdom. It is an honor to the king when his people multiply. It's a shame when his people are impoverished and dwindle away.

PRAY: *God honors me when my church, company or family grows. It's an honor.*

We grow because God thinks about us. We should become people whom God enjoys thinking about.

PSALM 115:12-16 (KJV)

12 The LORD hath been mindful of us: he will BLESS us; he will BLESS the house of Israel; he will BLESS the house of Aaron. **13** He will BLESS them that fear the LORD, both small and great. **14** The LORD shall INCREASE you more and more, you and your children. **15** Ye are BLESSED of the LORD which made heaven and earth. **16** The heaven, even the heavens, are the LORD's: but the earth hath he given to the children of men.

THE PROMISE OF LABORERS

MATTHEW 9:37-38 Then He said to His disciples, "The harvest truly is plentiful, but the laborers are few. **38** Therefore pray the Lord of the harvest to send out laborers into His harvest."

JEREMIAH 16:16 "Behold, I will send for many fishermen," says the Lord, "and they shall fish them; and afterward I will send for many hunters, and they shall hunt them from every mountain and every hill, and out of the holes of the rocks."

COMMENT: Jesus called us "fishers of men" in Mark 1:17 and Matthew 4:19. It refers to us catching sinners out of the pond of sin. Fishing in the Bible points to soul winning.

What if the fish won't bite? God said He will use a more aggressive tactic: He will send **hunters** to get His prize. Fishing is passive and peaceful compared to hunting. That means when sinners won't come to God in peace, He will turn up the heat. God will let them go through trials and tribulation so they turn away from the world and wake up to the Truth.

PRAY: *Heavenly Father, You said the harvest truly is plentiful, but the laborers are few. We pray the Lord of the Harvest to raise up more laborers and skilled helpers in our church—more fishers and hunters--experts in evangelism, IT, social media, outreach. Please send them into the harvest, the oceans, the mountains and hills, to catch Your People out of this world. Thrust all Christians out into the mission field, in Jesus' Name.*

· · ·

There are 5 main ways to increase.

1. INCREASE THROUGH THE ANOINTING

Growing in numbers is not the only way to grow a ministry. God can also increase a ministry through the Holy Spirit's Presence, Power (called the "Anointing"), Authority and Influence. This is just as real and as desirable as numerical increase.

ZECHARIAH 10:1 Ask the LORD for rain In the time of the latter rain. The LORD will make flashing clouds; He will give them showers of rain, Grass in the field for everyone.

HOSEA 6:3 [AKJ] Then shall we know, if we follow on to know the LORD: his going forth is prepared [or sure] as the morning; and he shall come to us as the rain, as the latter and former rain to the earth.

Pray: *Lord, give us the former and the latter rain that waters the harvest. Rain the gifts of the Holy Spirit on us. Let flashing clouds of Your Glory appear in our midst. Increase Your tangible anointing on my ministry, in Jesus' Name.*

2. INCREASE THROUGH MINISTRY

Another kind of growth that doesn't necessarily require growth in numbers is growing the scope or profile of ministry. A farmer doesn't necessarily benefit from having more workers. He may benefit more from adding variety to his existing farm: cattle, goats, sheep, chickens, fish or new fruit trees. He will harvest new products and fruits from adding variety to his farm.

Likewise we can add variety to our ministry activities: we can open up a street ministry, prayer clinic, prison outreach, hospital visitation, youth camps, children's church, or social activism, without adding more numbers to the church. Our members become stronger.

PROVERBS 14:4 Where no oxen are, the crib is clean: but much increase is by the strength of the ox.

PRAY: *Lord, we don't mind getting our hands dirty. Energize us to work for You. Increase us through the strength of workers.*

ACTS 11:23-24 Who [Barnabas], when he came, and had seen the grace of God, was glad, and exhorted them all, that with purpose of heart they would cleave unto the Lord. **24** For he was a good man, and full of the Holy Ghost and of faith: and much people was added unto the Lord.

PRAY: *Raise up more Barnabas's—good men and women who are full of the Holy Spirit and faith. Raise up people who celebrate others' success and encourage others to cleave to the Lord. Then add much people to us in Jesus' Name!*

Often we have to be better at team work and people skills before we are ready for addition and multiplication.

3. INCREASE THROUGH PRAISE AND WORSHIP

There's no doubt that growing churches have a high caliber worship team. This is the easiest way to grow a church numerically.

PSALM 22:3 (KJV) But thou art holy, O thou that inhabitest the praises of Israel.

The Japanese had a hard time translating this verse, so one of their Bible versions tells us this, "When you praise God, you make a throne for God to sit in." I like that.

JEREMIAH 30:19 And out of them shall proceed thanksgiving and the voice of them that make merry: and I will MULTIPLY them, and they shall not be few; I will also GLORIFY them, and they shall not be small.

JOHN 12:32 And I, if I be lifted up from the earth, will draw all men unto me.

There's a double entendre in this verse: 1) Jesus would be physically lifted up from the earth at His crucifixion, but also 2) We should lift Jesus up with our praises. Both actions draw all men to Jesus.

PSALM 40:3 (KJV) And he hath put a new song in my mouth, even praise unto our God: MANY shall see it, and fear, and shall trust in the LORD.

PRAY: *Father, put a new song in my mouth, that many will see it, fear You, and trust You. I lift up the Name of Your Son Jesus in song and praise. Please draw all men to Yourself every time they hear our worship. Add pure-hearted, talented worshippers to our team.*

ACTS 2:46-47 (KJV) And they, continuing daily with one accord in the temple, and breaking bread from house to house, did eat their meat with gladness and singleness of heart, **47** PRAISING God, and having favour with all the people. And the Lord ADDED to the church daily such as should be saved.

4. INCREASE THROUGH MIRACLES AND HEALING

ACTS 3:6-10, 4:4 (ESV) But Peter said, "I have no silver and gold, but what I do have I give to you. In the name of Jesus Christ of Nazareth, rise up and walk!" **7** And he took him by the right hand and raised him up, and immediately his feet and ankles were MADE STRONG… **9** And all the people saw him walking and praising God, **10** and recognized him as the one who sat at the Beautiful Gate of the temple, asking for alms. And they were filled with wonder and amazement at what had happened to him… **16** [Peter attributed the healing to Jesus' Name, not to his own apostleship. That alone disproves cessationism, the baseless claim that healing ceased with the original apostles. We have the same Name and same healing power as Peter had!] And His name, through faith in His name, has MADE this man STRONG, whom you see and know. Yes, the faith which comes through Him has given him this PERFECT SOUNDNESS in the presence of you all… 4:4 But MANY of those who had heard the word BELIEVED, and the number of the men came to about five thousand.

ACTS 5:12-14 (KJV) And by the hands of the apostles were many SIGNS and WONDERS wrought among the people; and they were all with one accord in Solomon's porch. And of the rest durst no man join himself to them: but the people magnified them. And believers were the more ADDED to the Lord, MULTITUDES both of men and women.

Pray: *Father, show us Your signs and wonders, miracles and healings, such that many people will believe and commit to a holy life of obedience and become active disciples in church, in Jesus' Name.*

5. INCREASE THROUGH MOMENTUM

Success breeds success. Growth produces more growth. "For whoever has, to him more will be given." (Mark 4:25) There's magic in momentum.

2 CHRONICLES 15:9 (NIV) Then he [King Asa] assembled all Judah and Benjamin and the people from Ephraim, Manasseh and Simeon who had settled among them, for LARGE NUMBERS had come over to him from Israel when they SAW that the Lord his God was with him.

People are attracted to *success*. Be careful about speaking down on yourself or trying to get people to feel sorry for you. You will attract the wrong kind of people—weak people and vultures who take advantage of others in their weakness.

Find the will of God and focus on it. Don't get distracted. Don't be jealous of others and say, "I see someone else succeed. I can do that, too." Stay in your gifting, calling and anointing. It is a delight to work with or be with someone who excels in what they love. You only need to excel in one or two things in life, and people will come. They will be drawn to your gift and feel attracted to you.

PROVERBS 22:9 Do you see a man who excels in his work? He will stand before kings; He will not stand before unknown men.

God graces you when you lock into your call and work at it diligently. Unfortunately some who are called to help love to lead. They get outside their calling and lose God's anointing. Some who are called to lead prefer not to have too much responsibility, too much pressure, too many demands. They act too passively to get momentum behind them.

You must learn to be the best "you" possible. If you stick with it, you will break through the veil, so to speak. Exponential growth, like Apple or Tesla experienced under Steve Jobs or Elon Musk, comes from a team of loyal people excelling and following a visionary leader. Even when they suffer setbacks, a core team of loyal, honorable people stick with the leader's vision. That's how breakthrough momentum comes.

Praying for your church to grow is one level of faith. You can step it up to the next level by praying for revival (which happens when many churches grow at the same time). See the chapter titled "Revival."

CHURCH GROWTH

WAYS I CAN ACTIVELY HELP GOD'S CHURCH GROW

14
CHURCH PROPERTY

We can confidently say the Lord has been good to us in one area: real estate. Our church is constantly blessed with the best properties.

One reason is that I have sown in this area. How do you sow towards land or building if you don't have a lot of money? I sowed towards other people's homes. I let them stay in my house for free or with minimal contribution towards bills. I never thought of making money from them. Within a year or two, several of them have saved up enough to buy their own homes. The harvest I've received has been greater than any rental income.

PSALM 37:11 (NAS) But the humble will **inherit the land,** and will delight themselves in abundant prosperity.

MARK 10:29-30 (KJV) And Jesus answered and said, Verily I say unto you, There is no man that hath left house, or brethren, or sisters, or father, or mother, or wife, or children, or lands, for my sake, and the gospel's, **30** But he shall receive an hundredfold **now in this time**, **houses**, and brethren, and sisters, and mothers, and children, and **lands**, with persecutions...

ISAIAH 65:21-22 (KJV) And **they shall build houses**, and inhabit them; and they shall plant vineyards, and eat the fruit of them. **22** They shall not build, and another inhabit; they shall not plant, and another eat: for as the days of a tree are the days of my people, and mine elect shall long enjoy the work of their hands.

CHURCH PROPERTY

DEUTERONOMY 6:10-11 "So it shall be, when the Lord your God brings you into the land of which He swore to your fathers, to Abraham, Isaac, and Jacob, to **give you** large and beautiful cities which you did not build, 11 **houses full of all good things**, which you did not fill…

DEUTERONOMY 11:23-25 (KJV) Then will the LORD drive out all these nations from before you, and ye shall possess greater nations and mightier than yourselves. **24 Every place** whereon the soles of your feet shall tread **shall be yours**: from the wilderness and Lebanon, from the river, the river Euphrates, even unto the uttermost sea shall your coast be. **25** There shall no man be able to stand before you: for the LORD your God shall lay the fear of you and the dread of you upon **all the land** that ye shall tread upon, as he hath said unto you.

BALANCE: *I did not say Christians can't rent out their homes. If you need to, do it. Charge sinners and sign a contract with them. I don't want to charge Christians because I want a different kind of harvest—one in which God repays our family in His own way.*

Note also, I let people stay rent-free for a year or more when I had only 1 child. Now that I have 4 children, I host guests for shorter periods of time, usually to help them move to a new area and get established.

15 COURT

> **LUKE 21:12-15** …You will be brought before kings and rulers for My name's sake. **13** But it will turn out for you as an occasion for testimony. **14** Therefore settle it in your hearts not to meditate beforehand on what you will answer; **15** for I will give you a mouth and wisdom which all your adversaries will not be able to contradict or resist.

Even good Christians go to court. It's not something we're to believe for, but if it happens, we are to be prepared. Do not be naïve. God told us a lot about His opinion of the human courts, judges and lawyers. Before the Ten Commandments, God gave Noah seven laws, minimal moral standards for humans, one of which was to "establish courts of justice." That is why we have courts today.

PROVERBS 29:26 Many seek the ruler's favor, But justice for man comes from the Lord.

You must accept that even though you pray for justice, justice may not come from the courts. Jesus did not get what He deserved in court, did He?

Jesus accepted the injustice done in human courts and trusted God the Father to bring about the best outcome. That is what Jesus got. He was vindicated by the resurrection after three days of death.

How to Conduct Yourself Before Trial

Jesus was so unconcerned about His court case that He "gave him [Pilate] no answer." (John 19:9) You will need to learn this principle to get the best possible outcome in court: *"Less is more."*

Don't talk too much, write too much, or answer too much. Don't try to justify yourself. Accept some wrong when it's honest to do so. The less you defend yourself the better.

Let someone else defend. Let your lawyer do the heavy lifting. Let the judge come to his own conclusions about you. Pilate said three times, "I find no fault in this Man concerning those things of which you accuse Him." (Luke 23:4, 14, John 19:6)

In other words, while accusations were flying, Jesus was not perturbed. For those who are innocent and try to live Christian lives, being falsely accused may seem like a gross insult that deserves to be countered or rebuffed. But accusations are "par for the course" in the game that worldly lawyers play every day. (The Christian lawyers I've met are little better.) They mudsling, throw dirt and hope it sticks. The judges see this every day and don't expect lawyers to be nice or do otherwise.

If you get involved and try to answer accusations, they will mock you for not knowing the rules of the game. Law is an insider sport. There is almost no truth in the secular court system. You can hear this in Pilate's tone when he looked at Jesus and said, **"What is truth?"** (John 18:38)

This was not a sincere question. This was a rhetorical one. This was not a *quest* for truth. This was, in fact, a *rejection* of truth. Pilate and all judges like him believe that the court system is not about truth. It's about lawyers making money by speaking in a way that's most pleasing to the ears of judges.

They are insiders; you are outsiders. Many judges enjoy taunting your ignorance. Never say to a judge, *"Your Honor, I'm not used to be being in court, so I may say something wrong."* It will only affirm what they think: you're an outsider.

ISAIAH 59:14-16 [NLT]

14 Our **courts oppose** the **righteous**, and justice is nowhere to be found. Truth stumbles in the streets, and honesty has been outlawed.

15 Yes, truth is gone, and anyone who renounces evil is attacked. The LORD looked and was displeased to find there was no justice.

16 He was amazed to see that no one intervened to help the oppressed. So he himself **stepped in to save them** with his strong arm, and his **justice** sustained him.

Praying for Justice on Earth

You must put your hope in God alone. Jesus is the Creator of Law and Justice, yet He was considered an outsider in the world's legal system. Jesus, even with all His rights and might, accepted He was an outsider. So He didn't bother to answer them at all.

> **LUKE 23:9** Then he [Herod] questioned Him with many words, but He answer him nothing. **10** And the chief priest and scribes stood and vehemently accused Him. **11** Then Herod, with his men of war, **treated Him with contempt** and mocked Him, arrayed Him in a gorgeous robe, and sent Him back to Pilate.

If you question the court, they call it "contempt of court." Yet you will rarely meet any human who holds ordinary people more in contempt than a secular judge. They treat innocent people like criminals—with no respect. They treated Jesus with contempt and mocked Him. Their formalities are usually pretense. They arrayed Him in a gorgeous robe, only to strip Him naked and crucify Him.

Jesus' only description of an earthly judge was recorded in the Gospel of Luke, "**Hear what the UNJUST judge said.**" (Luke 18:6) Those two words should form an oxymoron: "*unjust* judge." But that phrase describes most judges you'll meet. The wise and upright are few.

Do not be discouraged by this truth! Be *realistic* about humans and put your highest hopes on Jesus, not on the judge or justice system. Jesus promised justice to us in the next verse, "**And shall God not avenge His own elect who cry out day and night to Him, though He bears long with them?**" (Luke 18:7)

Why We Go Through Injustice

Justice is ours, but part of living a godly life and being a righteous person is to taste some injustice during our time on earth, just as our Lord tasted it for us.

No one has ever been more innocent than our Lord, yet no one has ever been treated more unjustly than Jesus. Two millennia later we look back at the story of Jesus and can tell all those Roman thugs were wrong. Their lives were failures, their names are forgotten, and their souls will be forever tormented in hell.

Jesus, on the other hand, was vindicated. His Church grew while the Romans Empire collapsed. His disciples are remembered while emperors are forgotten. His message outlasted Roman weapons and accomplished what Roman legions could not do: conquer the whole world. Jesus won!

ACTION: Once you believe justice ultimately comes from the Lord, it is OK to "sue for justice," to pursue justice, and to fight injustice wherever you meet it. But don't expect your answer to come only from the courts. Sometimes it comes in supernatural ways outside of court.

Praying Before Going to Court

Here are the Scriptures for you to pray the day before, the week before, or better yet, the month before your court date. Perhaps you're not heading to court, but facing a decision or evaluation from someone—a boss, business partner, investor, inspector, insurance adjuster, or committee—and things don't look favorable for you. These Scriptures that work for serious court cases will work for smaller cases, too.

TIP: Praying for justice is predicated on your innocence. I assume you are not guilty, but if you've disobeyed God in any way, you should repent out loud immediately. Do it where you're at. Don't delay.

You must not hold on to unconfessed sins and expect justice. Surrender to Jesus, forgive others, trust Him to wash you clean, and He will make you innocent in God's sight. Ask the Lord to save your life through Jesus Christ.

PRAY: *"Heavenly Father, I'm sorry for my sins. I'm sorry for hurting others. I believe Jesus died on the Cross to pay the penalty of my crimes, my mistakes, my sins. I believe after three days, Jesus rose again to new life. Jesus is not only the Son of God, but He's my Lord, Savior and King. Come make Your home in me and make me clean. Amen."*

These judicial prayers are for Christians only, because guilty people deserve punishment. Learn to cast your cares upon the Lord once you pray.

Stop Worrying. No Fear.

DEUTERONOMY 20:1 "When you go out to battle against your enemies, and see horses and chariots and people more numerous than you, do not be afraid of them; for the Lord your God is with you, who brought you up from the land of Egypt."

PHILIPPIANS 4:6 Do not be anxious about anything, but in everything by prayer and supplication with thanksgiving let your requests be made known to God.

PSALM 118:5-7 (HCSB) I called to the Lord in distress; the Lord answered me and put me in a spacious place. **6** The Lord is for me; I will not be afraid. What can man do to me? **7** The Lord is my helper, Therefore, I will look in TRIUMPH on those who hate me.

ROMANS 12:19 (NASB95) Never take your own revenge, beloved, but leave room for the wrath of God, for it is written, "VENGEANCE IS MINE, I WILL REPAY," says the Lord.

God Defends His Servants. Be His Servant.

PSALMS 119:65 (HCSB) LORD, You have treated Your **servant** well, just as You promised.

(NET) You are good to your **servant**, O LORD, just as you promised.

ISAIAH 54:17 No weapon formed against you shall prosper, And every tongue which rises against you in judgment You shall condemn. This is the heritage of the **servants of the Lord**, And their righteousness is from Me," Says the Lord.

PSALMS 113:7-8 (KJV) He raiseth up the poor out of the dust, and lifteth the needy out of the dunghill; **8** That he may set him with princes, even with the princes of his people. [Written about His servants Joseph and David—a promise to those who serve.]

Pray for justice the right way, stop worrying, then leave it up to God how He wants to vindicate you. He may guide a judge's mind or He may override a judge altogether. He can do it.

ISAIAH 40:23 He brings the princes to nothing; He makes the judges of the earth useless.

Our salvation does not come from judges. Our faith is not in lawyers, though God can use them. When we humble ourselves before God's Son, we will win in the end. Truth will prevail. Justice must be served, because God is watching everything done by everyone.

Proceed to the chapters on "Justice" and "Lawsuits & Legal Battles" for Scriptures to apply and pray. Don't worry. God's Word works!

16
DELIVERANCE

These Scriptures promise your deliverance from bondage, fear, oppression, and evil.

MATTHEW 6:13 And do not lead us into temptation, But deliver us from the evil one. For Yours is the kingdom and the power and the glory forever. Amen.

PSALM 140:1 Deliver me, O Lord, from evil men; preserve me from violent men.

PSALM 37

1 Do not fret because of evildoers, Nor be envious of the workers of iniquity.

2 For they shall soon be **cut down like the grass**, And wither as the green herb.

3 Trust in the Lord, and do good; Dwell in the land, and feed on His faithfulness.

4 Delight yourself also in the Lord, And He shall give you the desires of your heart.

5 Commit your way to the Lord, Trust also in Him, And He shall bring it to pass.

DELIVERANCE

6 He shall bring forth your righteousness as the light, And your justice as the noonday.

7 Rest in the Lord, and wait patiently for Him; **Do not fret** because of him who prospers in his way, Because of the man who brings wicked schemes to pass.

8 Cease from anger, and forsake wrath; **Do not fret**—it only causes harm.

9 For evildoers shall be cut off; But those who wait on the Lord, They shall inherit the earth.

10 For yet **a little while and the wicked shall be no more**; Indeed, **you will look carefully for his place, But it shall be no more**.

23 The steps of a good man are ordered by the Lord, And He delights in his way.

24 Though he fall, he shall not be utterly cast down; For the Lord upholds him with His hand.

25 I have been young, and now am old; Yet I have not seen the righteous forsaken, Nor his descendants begging bread.

35 I have seen the wicked in great power, And spreading himself like a native green tree.

36 Yet he passed away, and behold, he was **no more**; Indeed I sought him, but he could not be found.

37 Mark the blameless man, and observe the upright; For the future of that man is peace.

38 But the transgressors shall be destroyed together; The future of the wicked shall be cut off.

39 But the salvation of the righteous is from the Lord; He is their strength in the time of trouble.

40 And the Lord shall help them and **deliver** them; He shall **deliver** them from the wicked, And save them, Because they trust in Him.

Psalm 37 is my favorite psalm of deliverance. The first condition of deliverance is found in verse 1, *"Do not fret because of evil doers."* That means don't worry. It's repeated in verses 7 and 8. *"Do not fret."* If you trust God, you won't worry.

PSALM 37:5-10 (NET)

5 Commit your future to the LORD! Trust in him, and he will act on your behalf. **6** He will vindicate you in broad daylight, and publicly defend your just cause. **7** Wait patiently for the LORD! Wait confidently for him! Do not fret over the apparent success of a sinner, a man who carries out wicked schemes! **8** Do not be angry and frustrated! Do not fret! That only leads to trouble! **9** Wicked men will be wiped out, but those who rely on the LORD are the ones who will possess the land. **10** Evil men will soon disappear; you will stare at the spot where they once were, but they will be gone.

If we don't worry, what are we supposed to do? Verse 5 instructs us, "Commit your way to the Lord, Trust also in Him, And He shall bring it to pass." The New English Translation (NET) says, "Commit your future to the Lord! Trust in him, and he will act on your behalf."

If we want God to act on our behalf, we must follow His command. The New Testament tells us to stop worrying: *"Casting all your care upon him; for he careth for you."* (1 Peter 5:7) To cast means to throw far away from you. God wants you to cast your cares upon Him, put the matter in His hands, then accept His deliverance before you feel it.

PRAISE FOR DELIVERANCE

Hannah and David sang the same words when they were delivered from oppression. Hannah was tormented by her "sister wife" Peninnah (the other wife of her husband Eli). When Hannah was delivered from her struggle and shame, she sang the following, which I use for my own prayer of deliverance:

1 SAMUEL 2:8 (GNT) He lifts the poor from the dust and raises the needy from their misery. He makes them companions of princes and puts them in places of honor.

1 SAMUEL 2:8 (MEV) He raises up the poor out of the dust and lifts up the oppressed from the dunghill to make them sit with princes and inherit a throne of glory.

DELIVERANCE

PRAY: *The Lord lifts me from the dust and raises me from my misery. He makes me a companion of princes, presidents, prime ministers, prophets, pastors and puts me in places of honor.*

1 SAMUEL 2:8-9 (ISV) He raises the poor up from the dust, he lifts up the needy from the trash heap to make them sit with princes and inherit a seat of honor. Indeed the pillars of the earth belong to the Lord, and he has set the world on them. **9** He guards the steps of his faithful ones, while the wicked are made silent in darkness. He grants the request of the one who prays. He blesses the year of the righteous. Indeed it's not by strength that a person prevails.

PRAY: *My Heavenly Father guards my steps, while the wicked are sitting in silence and darkness. They are confused and don't know what to do. He grants my request whenever I pray. He blesses my year because I am the righteousness of God in Christ. I will prevail, triumph and overcome. I will have a victory and praise report everyone will know about, just like Hannah!*

Decades later, David was tormented by King Saul and his informant Doeg the Edomite (1 Samuel 21-22). When David was delivered and lifted high above his enemies, David sang this praise:

PSALMS 113:7-9 (KJV) He raiseth up the poor out of the dust, and lifteth the needy out of the dunghill; **8** That he may set him with princes, even with the princes of his people. **9** He maketh the barren woman to keep house, and to be a joyful mother of children. Praise ye the LORD.

Verse 9 may not seem to be connected to verse 8, until you realize that both are related to his life. Hannah was the barren mother who bore the prophet Samuel who anointed David to be king.

PRAY: *He raises me the poor out of the dust, and lifts me the needy out of the dunghill, that He may set me with princes, even with the princes of His people. He makes my wife to keep house, and to be a joyful mother of my children.*

Lord, I don't want to miss out on anything You do. Please put me in the most anointed events among the most anointed people whom You love. Don't let me waste time being with people who look good on the outside, but don't enjoy being with You and You don't enjoy being with them. Raise me out of the dust of mediocrity and lift me out of the dunghill of unholy celebrities, O Lord, in Jesus' Name!

GET PRAYERS ANSWERED

Did you know that Jesus also sang this Psalm? It is Jewish tradition to sing Psalm 113 at the blessing of the first Passover cup. This means that Jesus sung this Psalm on the night before He was crucified. Jesus sang it by faith, expecting to be lifted out of a literal ash heap. If He sang it by faith, before being resurrected, we can also appropriate this by faith.

> **PSALM 113:7-8** (ESV) He raises the poor from the dust and lifts the needy from the ash heap, **8** to make them sit with princes, with the princes of his people.

If Jesus sang this by faith, before His resurrection, we can sing it and pray it, too. We receive it by faith. Imagine how much power is contained in these words.

STEP 1: ACT. I cast my cares on You, Lord, by writing them here.

_____

_____

_____

_____

STEP 2: SAY, *I cast my cares upon the Lord for He cares for me. The entire matter is now in Your Hands. I am no longer concerned, even though it concerns me. I delight myself in the Lord, and He gives me the desires of my heart. I commit my ways to the Lord, I trust also in Him, and He has brought it to pass. He is acting on my behalf now, in Jesus' Name.*

_____

_____

_____

_____

See related topics in chapters on "Sexual Purity" and "Temptation."

17

DIFFICULT PEOPLE

The 3 Best Prayers for Difficult People

The most powerful prayers in the New Testament are the prayers that the Apostle Paul prayed for other Christians. They're inspired by the Holy Spirit. They're already anointed. So they're guaranteed to get answered.

This is how Paul prayed for believers in Ephesus. Paul did not pray that God would give more, but that they would grow up spiritually and mature in their understanding of what Jesus already did for them. We should pray exactly this way, substituting "you" with the name of someone

> **EPHESIANS 1:15-22** (NKJV) Therefore I also, after I heard of your faith in the Lord Jesus and your love for all the saints, **16** do not cease to give thanks for you, making mention of you in my prayers: **17** that the God of our Lord Jesus Christ, the Father of glory, may give to you the spirit of wisdom and revelation in the knowledge of Him, **18** the eyes of your understanding being enlightened; that you may know what is the hope of His calling, what are the riches of the glory of His inheritance in the saints, **19** and what is the exceeding greatness of His power toward us who believe, according to the working of His mighty power **20** which He worked in

Christ when He raised Him from the dead and seated Him at His right hand in the heavenly places, **21** far above all principality and power and might and dominion, and every name that is named, not only in this age but also in that which is to come. **22** And He put all things under His feet, and gave Him to be head over all things to the church, **23** which is His body, the fullness of Him who fills all in all.

Ephesians chapter 3 is even clearer than Ephesians chapter 1 about the goal Paul had in mind when praying for others. The ultimate goal of prayer is that Christians would discern the will of God, walk in the calling of God, and fulfill their destiny in Christ. It's very powerful to pray for ourselves or for others like Paul prayed for the Ephesians in chapter 3.

> **EPHESIANS 3:13-21** Therefore I ask [pray] that you do not lose heart at my tribulations for you, which is your glory. **14** For this reason I bow my knees to the Father of our Lord Jesus Christ, **15** from whom the whole family in heaven and earth is named, **16** that He would grant you, according to the riches of His glory, to **be strengthened** with might through His Spirit in the inner man, **17** that Christ may dwell in your hearts through faith; that you, **being rooted and grounded in love**, **18** may be able to **comprehend** with all the saints what *is* the width and length and depth and height — **19** to **know** the love of Christ which passes knowledge; that you may **be filled** with all the fullness of God. **20** Now to Him who is able to do exceedingly abundantly above all that we ask or think, according to the **power** that works **in us, 21** to Him *be* glory in the church by Christ Jesus to all generations, forever and ever. Amen.

Paul did not write a letter to the Ephesian believers with chapters and verses. Those were added later. If I had numbered the sentences, I would *not* have separated the end of chapter 3 from the beginning of chapter 4, as they cover the same topic. Let's continue to pray the inspired words of Paul.

> **EPHESIANS 4:1-6** I, therefore, the prisoner of the Lord, beseech [pray for] you to walk worthy of **the calling** with which you were called [how?], **2** with all lowliness and gentleness, with longsuffering, bearing with one another in love, **3** endeavoring to keep the unity of the Spirit in the bond of peace. [Why?] **4** There is one body and one Spirit, just as you were called in one hope of your calling; **5** one Lord, one faith, one baptism; **6** one God and Father of all, who is above all, and through all, and in you all.

Ephesians and Colossians are known as *"sister epistles."* So it should come as no surprise that Colossians contains a similar prayer as the above Ephesian prayers. I also like to pray this for others.

> **COLOSSIANS 1:9-14** For this reason we also, since the day we heard it, do not cease to pray for you, and to ask that you may be filled with the knowledge of His will in all wisdom and spiritual understanding; **10** that you may walk worthy of the Lord, fully pleasing *Him,* being **fruitful in every good work and increasing in the knowledge of God**; **11** strengthened with all might, according to His glorious power, for all patience and longsuffering with joy; **12** giving thanks to the Father who has qualified us to be partakers of the inheritance of the saints in the light. **13** **He has delivered us from the power of darkness** and conveyed *us* into the kingdom of the Son of His love, **14** in whom **we have redemption** through His blood, the forgiveness of sins.

If our eyes were opened to the above redemptive reality, nothing would defeat us. God is in us! His power and peace dwell in us. He saved us for His purpose and called us to a holy calling. I pray you understand and walk out His will as soon as possible!

For more Scriptures to pray for others, go to the chapter titled "Leaders."

18 ELECTION

Prayer for Honest Elections and a Change in Government

On what basis can we believe for a reform at governmental level? Here are 6 Scriptures that tell us God is interested in politics. There is no "separation of Church and State" for God. He wants to depose wicked rulers and establish just ones over us. He is waiting for us to ask Him!

PSALM 75:6-7 (KJV)

6 For promotion cometh neither from the east, nor from the west, nor from the south.

7 But God is the judge: he putteth down one, and setteth up another.

PROVERBS 29:2 (KJV) When the righteous are in authority, the people rejoice: but when the wicked beareth rule, the people mourn.

LUKE 1:51-52 [NIV — Mary's prayer]

51...he has scattered those who are proud in their inmost thoughts.

52 He has brought down rulers from their thrones but has lifted up the humble.

(ISV) **52** He pulled powerful rulers from their thrones and lifted up humble people.

ELECTION

(NET) **52** He has brought down the mighty from their thrones & has lifted up those of lowly position.

LUKE 1:74 [Zechariah's prayer] That he would grant unto us, that we being delivered out of the hand of our enemies might serve him without fear

COMMENT: The longing of Zechariah, the father of John the Baptist, is my longing…that we should be delivered out of the hand of our enemies so that we may serve Jesus without fear.

PRAY: *May all our enemies be dethroned, arrested and replaced by Godly rulers, so that we can serve Jesus freely and without fear. Our freedom has a purpose: it's service!*

DANIEL 4:37 Now I, Nebuchadnezzar, praise and extol and honor the King of heaven, all of whose works are truth, and His ways justice. And those who walk in pride He is able to put down.

(KJV) …those that walk in pride he is able to abase.

PRAY: *Heavenly Father, You humbled the proudest ruler of the most powerful empire. How much more You will humble our leaders, pastors, senators, congressmen, judges, governors, presidents, prime ministers, premiers, and businessmen. Humble them till they praise and extol and honor the King of Heaven, and acknowledge that Your works are truth and Your ways are justice, in Jesus' Name I pray. Amen.*

PSALM 113:7-9

7 He raises the poor out of the dust, And lifts the needy out of the ash heap [KJV says 'dunghill'],

8 That He may seat him with princes— With the princes of His people.

9 He grants the barren woman a home, Like a joyful mother of children. Praise the Lord!

PRAY: *Lord, You were able to raise Joseph out of obscurity and to the most prominent position in Egypt. Would You raise up qualified Christians to lead this world out of chaos and into revival? Raise humble Christians out of the dust and lift me as one of those needy out of the dunghill, that You may seat us with princes —with the princes of Your people! Grant us a spiritual home and make us joyful seeing our spiritual children multiply into a tribe, in Jesus' Name I pray.*

19
EMOTIONS

Depression is a big issue these days. It didn't used to be this way. One big cause is people now don't realize how blessed they are and how much they have.

Another trigger for depression is feeling pressured by situations that we cannot control. The end of a relationship is often beyond our control and can lead some people to depression. But this implies good things can also lead some people to depression. For instance, having a baby can lead some women to depression. It's very hard to control a baby or a child.

In the past, traditional mothers got depressed because they could not control the gender of a child. They were expected to have a boy, but they got a girl. It was outside of their control. It was in fact determined not by her at all, but solely by her husband's sperm contributing the deciding X or Y chromosome. Even though scientifically it was not her fault, it was still out of her control. The two results of feeling out of control were: the mother got depressed and she sent the spirit of rejection into her newborn child.

If you think about things you cannot control, you will be depressed and even suicidal. Know this: the devil will use evil, good, and our own forgetfulness to stir up our emotions. He'll use everything! Let's not be "ignorant of his devices." (2 Corinthians 2:11) Remind yourself: you are not meant to be in charge of everything; let God be in charge of your life, and you'll be free and at peace.

Even if you're a righteous person, you will be tested by people and circumstances beyond your control. You will have to pass this test. Many are the afflictions of the righteous, but the Lord delivers him out of them all. (Psalm 34:19)

When we feel rejected or betrayed, we don't have to be up and down emotionally. I know because I used to get depressed before Christ saved me. But I have not been depressed since I got born again and Spirit-filled. That was 30 years ago. I want to show you the secret of how to be balanced emotionally.

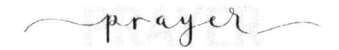

prayer

1 TIMOTHY 6:6-10

6 Now godliness with CONTENTMENT is great gain.

7 For we brought nothing into this world, and it is certain we can carry nothing out.

8 And having food and clothing, with these we shall be CONTENT.

9 But those who desire to be rich fall into temptation and a snare, and into many foolish and harmful lusts which drown men in destruction and perdition.

10 For the LOVE of MONEY is a root of all kinds of EVIL, for which some have strayed from the faith in their greediness, and pierced themselves through with many sorrows.

COMMENT: Being content is the secret to never being depressed. A content person focuses on the positive rather than the negative. Contentment is worth more than gold.

The opposite of contentment is the love of money, greed and jealousy. Jealousy is a form of feeling out of control. One person sees another person has what they want and can't have, so they feel it's out of their control. To control, they either have to work hard for the god of money or they have to destroy the person who has what they can't have. Such Satanic feelings can lead to murder.

If money or jealousy motivates you in ministry, you will eventually fail and feel depressed. You must have a bigger goal in life than making more money than someone else or being more popular than someone else. You should be content with God's plan for you.

LUKE 3:14 Likewise the soldiers asked him [John the Baptist], saying, "And what shall we do?" So he said to them, "Do not intimidate anyone or accuse falsely, and be CONTENT with your wages."

PHILIPPIANS 4:11-13

11 Not that I speak in regard to need, for I have learned in whatever state I am, to be CONTENT:

12 I know how to be abased, and I know how to abound. Everywhere and in all things I have learned both to be full and to be hungry, both to abound and to suffer need.

13 I can do all things through Christ who strengthens me.

PHILIPPIANS 4:8-9 (KJV)

8 Finally, brethren, whatsoever things are TRUE, whatsoever things are HONEST, whatsoever things are JUST, whatsoever things are PURE, whatsoever things are LOVELY, whatsoever things are of GOOD report; if there be any virtue, and if there be any praise, THINK on these things.

9 Those things, which ye have both learned, and received, and heard, and seen in me, do: and the God of PEACE shall be with you.

COUNTING MY BLESSINGS

SAY: *I choose to focus on what I have rather than what I don't. I fear God and remind myself that life can get a lot worse if I stay discontented. I am grateful for:*

_____

_____

_____

_____

_____

20
ENEMIES

Modern Christians know how to pray *for* their enemies, but they have forgotten how to pray *against* their enemies. Jesus said, *"Love your enemies, bless those who curse you, do good to those who hate you, and pray for those who spitefully use you and persecute you"* (Matthew 5:44). After having said this, Jesus forgave a woman caught in the act of adultery (John 8) on one instance; and in another instance, Jesus whipped his enemies who turned His Father's "House of Prayer" into a "den of thieves" (Luke 19:46). In both instances, Jesus was loving to His enemies.

Why were His reactions so different? In the first instance, the humiliated woman showed repentance, so Love extended grace to her. In the second instance, the thieves operating in God's Temple were hardened sinners, so Love extended to them punishment. Jesus did what was best for each of them, and for other people involved, in that situation.

I FORGIVE & GIVE TO GOD PEOPLE WHO ACT LIKE MY ENEMIES:

_____
_____
_____
_____

ROMANS 16:20 (NASB) The God of peace will soon crush Satan under your feet. The grace of our Lord Jesus be with you.

PROVERBS 16:7 When a man's ways please the Lord, He makes even his **enemies** to be at peace with him.

ISAIAH 54:15 (AMPC) Behold, they may gather together and stir up strife, but it is not from Me. Whoever stirs up strife against you shall **fall** and **surrender** to you."

PSALMS 86:17 (NIV) Give me a sign of your goodness, that my **enemies** may see it and be put to **shame**, for you, LORD, have helped me and comforted me.

PSALM 23:5-6 You prepare a table before me **in the presence of my enemies**; You anoint my head with oil; My cup runs over. **6** Surely goodness and mercy shall follow me All the days of my life; And I will dwell in the house of the Lord Forever.

REVELATION 3:9 Indeed I will make those of the synagogue of Satan, who say they are Jews and are not, but lie—indeed **I will make them** come and worship before your feet, and to **know that I have loved you**.

PSALMS 109:29 (KJV) 29 Let mine **adversaries** be clothed with shame, and let them cover themselves with their own confusion, as with a mantle.

PSALMS 41:10,11 (NLT) LORD, have mercy on me. Make me well again, so I can pay them back! **11** I know you are pleased with me, for you have not let my **enemies** triumph over me.

(Aramaic) **11** In this I have known that you are pleased with me, because my **enemy** does not harm me.

PSALMS 35:26-27 (KJV) Let them be ashamed and brought to confusion together that rejoice at mine hurt: let them be clothed with shame and dishonour that magnify themselves **against me**. **27** Let them shout for joy, and be glad, that favour my righteous cause: yea, let them say continually, Let the LORD be magnified, which hath pleasure in the prosperity of his servant.

ENEMIES

1 CORINTHIANS 5:4-5 (NKJ) In the name of our Lord Jesus Christ, when you are gathered together, along with my spirit, with the power of our Lord Jesus Christ, **5** deliver **such a one** to Satan for the destruction of the flesh, that his spirit may be saved in the day of the Lord Jesus.

MICAH 7:8-10 (KJV) Rejoice not against me, O mine enemy: when I fall, I shall arise; when I sit in darkness, the LORD shall be a light unto me. **9** I will bear the indignation of the LORD, because I have sinned against him, until he **plead my cause**, and **execute judgment for me**: he will bring me forth to the LIGHT, and I shall behold his righteousness. **10** Then she that is mine enemy shall see it, and shame shall cover her which said unto me, Where is the LORD thy God? mine eyes shall behold her: now shall she be trodden down as the mire of the streets.

ISAIAH 10:33 ….Those of high stature [like judges, doctors, bankers] will be hewn down. And the **haughty** will be humbled. [God will punish the dangerous use of judicial authority.]

ISAIAH 12:11 I will punish the world for its evil, and the wicked for their iniquity; I will halt the arrogance of the **proud** [like social critics, online bullies], and will lay low the haughtiness of the terrible [or tyrants].

ISAIAH 14:3-7 It shall come to pass in the day the Lord gives you REST from your SORROW, and from your FEAR and HARD BONDAGE in which you were made to serve, **4** that you will take up this proverb against the **king of Babylon** [your enemy], and say: "How the oppressor has ceased, the golden city ceased! **5** The Lord has broken the staff of the **wicked**, the scepter of the **rulers** [or bosses or judges]… **7** The whole earth is at rest and quiet; They break forth into singing.

ISAIAH 17:14…And before morning, he [the trouble maker] is no more. This is the portion of those who **plunder** us, And the lot of those who **rob** us.

ISAIAH 37:20 Now therefore, O LORD our God, save us from his hand, that all the kingdoms of the earth may know that You are the LORD, You alone.

COMMENT: Call for the end of your enemy if they've shown no desire for repentance or reconciliation. The purpose of this prayer is to show God's justice and save the innocent from prolonged injustice.

ISAIAH 33:19 You will not see a fierce people…

SAY: *I will finally dwell with peaceful, gentle, quiet spirits.*

ISAIAH 40:23 He brings the **princes** to nothing; He makes the **judges** of the earth useless.

ISAIAH 42:1, 3-4, 6-7, 9 (brackets […] denotes my comments)

1 Behold! My Servant whom I uphold, My Elect One in whom My soul delights! I have put My Spirit upon Him; He will bring forth JUSTICE to the **Gentiles**.

3 … He [Jesus] will bring forth JUSTICE for truth.

4 He will not fail nor be discouraged [that implies there will be setbacks along the path to justice], till He has established JUSTICE in the earth… [justice takes time—it will require of you patience, but God is working!]

7 To open blind eyes [like the judge's or jurors' eyes], To bring out prisoners from the prison, Those who sit in darkness from the prison house [note the Messiah's mission and anointing are to deal with judicial matters or issues of justice]…

9 Behold, the former things have come to pass [or are already past], And new things [new orders, new decisions, new laws] I declare; Before they spring forth I tell you of them.

ISAIAH 44:25 Who frustrates the signs of the **babblers** [lawyers], and drives **diviners** [judges] mad: Who turns wise men backward, and makes their knowledge foolishness; 26 Who confirms the word of His servant, and performs the counsel of His messengers [ministers].

COMMENT: Your enemies in court will be frustrated. Lawyers are talkers or babblers. Judges are like fortune tellers; they tell people's future by their assumptions and court orders. God will not confirm their words. Rather He will confirm the word or counsel of His servants. When you serve the Lord, you have this protection from babbles and diviners!

ISAIAH 49:19 …And those who **swallowed** you up will be far away.

ISAIAH 54:15…Whoever **assembles against** you shall fall for your sake.

ENEMIES

ISAIAH 54:17 No **weapon formed** against you shall prosper, and every **tongue** which **rises against** you in judgment you shall condemn. This is the heritage of the servants of the Lord, and their righteousness is from me," says the Lord.

COMMENT: There is a special promise of protection that is exclusive to "servants of the Lord," meaning not every Christian experiences this level of persecution on the one hand, and this level of covering on the other. The higher the call, the bigger the enemy, and the more glorious the deliverance.

GOD TROUBLES THE WICKED

ISAIAH 47:10-11 [speaking of Israel's enemy Babylon] For you have trusted in your wickedness; You have said, 'No one sees me'; Your wisdom and your knowledge have warped you…**11** Therefore **evil shall come upon you**; You shall not know from where it arises. And **trouble shall fall** upon you; You will not be able to put it off. And desolation shall come upon you suddenly, Which you shall not know.

COMMENT: One of the sure promises of the Bible is that your enemies have enemies, and they will fight each other and consume each other without your prompting. You just believe, pray and obey.

ISAIAH 48:32 "There is no peace," says the LORD, "for the wicked." [What is there for them instead? Justice!]

ISAIAH 50:7-9, 11

7 For the Lord God will help Me; Therefore I will not be disgraced; Therefore I have set My face like a flint, And I know that I will not be ashamed. **8** He is near who justifies Me; Who will contend with Me?… **9** Surely the Lord God will help Me; Who is he who will condemn Me? Indeed they will all **grow old** like a garment… [A critical spirit ages faster than normal. They will have extra lines on their face and poor health. They will grow old like a garment, which doesn't last long. Time will show the insides of a person.]

11 Look, all you who kindle a fire…This you shall have from My hand: You shall lie down in torment. [Your enemies shall suffer torment. They who send fire with their mouths will have fire come back to them. They are under a Curse!]

"ENJOY THE PROCESS"

Many years ago when I faced a difficult trial in my life, the Lord spoke to me, *"Enjoy the process."* Sometimes there's a delay in your life and there's nothing you can do about it, because God is working on someone else's heart, waiting for their obedience, extending mercy over their disobedience. You often don't have the complete picture when you're going through a waiting season or painful period. It's not always about you. Enjoy the process.

The Scriptures below helped me have strength while waiting for answers.

JOEL 3:10 (NIV) Beat your plowshares into swords and your pruning hooks into spears. Let the weakling say, "I am strong!"

ROMANS 8:37 No, in all these things we are more than conquerors through him who loved us.

2 CORINTHIANS 2:14 (NAS) But thanks be to God, who always leads us in triumph in Christ, and manifests through us the sweet aroma of the knowledge of Him in every place.

JOHN 16:33 (ESV) I have said these things to you, that in me you may have peace. In the world you will have tribulation. But take heart; I have overcome the world.

FORGIVE ME FOR WORRYING ABOUT:

_____

_____

_____

_____

You will find more Scriptures about enemies in the chapters "Pride" and "Protection." To pray for Biblical Justice against scammers and get restoration from a loss, read my prayer book:
SCAM PROOF YOUR LIFE IN THE END TIMES *,†

---

* Paperback: https://amzn.to/3u3Q6Ag
† Kindle: https://amzn.to/3u01ywS

21
EVANGELISM

Evangelism, speaking to strangers about their eternal destinies, is one of the most difficult things for most people. People avoid it because it somehow brings fear in their hearts. The same people will not hesitate to recommend to others a restaurant, a movie or something as expensive as an electric car. To overcome this irrational fear when speaking about your favorite person—Jesus—you should meditate on these Scriptures from time to time. They will help you regain your confidence. God loves it when you are bold for Him!

ACTS 26 Confession [Jesus appeared to Paul and gave him a commission. My mission is similar to Paul's mission.]

16 But rise and stand on your feet; for I have appeared to you for this purpose, to make you a minister and a witness both of the things which you have seen and of the things which I will yet reveal to you.

17 I will deliver you from the Jewish people, as well as from the Gentiles, to whom I now send you,

18 to open their eyes, in order to turn them from darkness to light, and from the power of Satan to God, that they may receive forgiveness of sins and an inheritance among those who are sanctified by faith in Me.'

. . .

The 5-Fold Commission: Jesus sends me to the Gentiles [Africans/ Arabs/ Asians/ Europeans/ Jews/ Latinos/ name your people group _____] to

1. open their eyes
2. turn them from darkness to light
3. from the power of Satan to God
4. that they may receive forgiveness of sins, and
5. an inheritance among those who are sanctified by faith in Jesus.

ACTS 26:19-20

19 "Therefore, King Agrippa, I was not disobedient to the heavenly vision,

20 but declared first to those in Damascus and in Jerusalem, and throughout all the region of Judea, and then to the Gentiles, that they should repent, turn to God, and do works befitting repentance.

The 3-Fold Message: I declare to people that they should

1. repent
2. turn to God, and
3. do works meet for repentance (show proof of repentance).

ACTS 26:22 Therefore, having obtained help from God, to this day I stand, witnessing both to small and great, saying no other things than those which the prophets and Moses said would come.

The 2-Fold Audience: Having obtained the help of God, I continue to this day, witnessing to both

1. small and
2. great.

ACTS 26:22b-23 ...saying no other things than those which the prophets and Moses said would come— **23** that the Christ would suffer, that He would be the first to rise from the dead, and would proclaim light to the Jewish people and to the Gentiles."

. . .

The 3 Great Guarantees: I say no other things than

1. those which the prophets and Moses say should come (All Bible prophecy is guaranteed to come to pass)
2. that Christ should suffer (The full payment for all our sins is guaranteed), and
3. that He should be the FIRST to rise from the dead (The resurrection is guaranteed. Since Christ was the first to be resurrected, we have a guarantee all men will be resurrected).

ACTS 26:24-27

24 Now as he thus made his defense, Festus said with a loud voice, "Paul, you are beside yourself! Much learning is driving you mad!" **25** But he said, "I am not mad, most noble Festus, but speak the words of truth and reason. **26** For the king, before whom I also speak freely, knows these things; for I am convinced that none of these things escapes his attention, since this thing was not done in a corner. **27** King Agrippa, do you believe the prophets? I know that you do believe." **28** Then Agrippa said to Paul, "You almost persuade me to become a Christian."

The 2-Fold Defense:

1. I am not mad, but
2. speak forth the words of truth and soberness (reason). I speak what is true and reasonable (NIV). I speak the sober truth (RSV, NAS, TLB). Acts 26:25

Was Paul a madman? If he was mad, we should not follow him. If he was not, all should listen to him. Notice the twisted mentality of the world: Paul was not called a mad man when he was murdering Christians; only after he admitted Jesus was right and he was wrong did the world call him mad. Why is that? The world is mad. When we worship the Creator and obey His Son, we grow in sanity.

ACTS 26:29 And Paul said, "I would to God that not only you, but also ALL who hear me today, might become both almost and altogether such as I am, except for these chains."

(God's Word) Paul replied, "I wish to God that you and everyone listening to me today would quickly and completely become as I am (except for being a prisoner)."

The Compassion & All-Inclusive Invitation of the Gospel

Paul said in his defense: I would to God that not only you, but also ALL that hear me this day, were both almost and ALTOGETHER such as I am.

How many men can say, "Be almost and altogether such as I am?"

How many men can say, "Follow me as I follow Christ?"

How many can say, "Imitate me" (1 Corinthians 11:1)?

A just and righteous man can.

ACTION: Go call everybody to be just like you! Go evangelize!

PEOPLE / NATIONS I WILL EVANGELIZE

_____

_____

_____

_____

_____

_____

_____

_____

_____

_____

22
FAMILY

Prayers for family situations have been separated into the following chapters:

- *6 Steps to Save Your Family* — the most important steps to follow to see your family saved and serving the Lord.
- *Apostles' Creed* — a confession of faith that you can do with your children so they grow up believing the core tenets of Christianity. Don't assume they know it. Don't rely on their school or church to teach it to them.
- *Children* — prayers for children and teenagers to grow up loving God and serving Him; plus Scriptures for parents to be empowered.
- *Eating* — how to say "grace" before eating. We taught our babies to say grace as soon as they could speak. They thanked God for their milk.
- *Enemies* — There are 4 things every child of God must learn in the proper order: 1) Who their father is, 2) Who they are in Christ, 3) Who their enemy is, and 4) How to express sincere thanks from their heart, especially towards God our Savior (aka worship). One of the things Jewish parents teach their children better than Christian parents—and I believe this is the key to their success...rarely do they have a child who is ashamed of their Jewish heritage or renounces their faith—is they constantly remind their

children that the Jews have enemies. Jesus warns us about mockers and persecutors, but Christian parents rarely talk about them. This chapter teaches Christians how to deal with enemies in a Biblical way.
- *Goals & Priorities* — at least once a year we encourage every family member to revisit their previous year's goals and dreams, and to write down and illustrate on a big piece of paper we call a "Dream Board" their new goals and dreams for the next year. Our children have had amazing results.
- *Home Dedication* — prayer to bless the physical house you live in.
- *Houses to the Godly* — prayer for first home ownership and growth in real estate.
- *Lord's Prayer* — an essential prayer for all families to memorize and pray together. According to Jesus, it is a model—a pattern of how to pray and what to pray for in which order. So we sometimes elaborate on each line to apply to our specific circumstances.
- *Morning Praise* — this is what I pray in the morning by myself; consequently, my children have also begun to copy what I say.
- *Pastors* —we teach children to respect God and His servants by inviting them to pray for pastors. Never badmouth your pastor. Parents who do eventually lose their children because they undermine their own authority when they undermine God's authority.
- *Pregnancy* — prayer to conceive a child.
- *Sexual Purity* — a faith-filled pledge for anyone in your family tempted with pornography or other sexual sin.
- *Sleep* — prayer for a goodnight sleep. This works for young and old.
- *Sabbath Blessing* — a model to bless your children's identity at family meals and/or during Shabbat.
- *Warfare Prayer* — the prayer I prayed the most often. My older children have started to copy me in this habit.

MY FAMILY NOTES

23
FAMINE

Nearly every generation experienced a famine in the Bible. Believe it or not, just like in modern times, some people prospered during famines. Such were the cases of Isaac and Joseph—they got better.

My prayer is that you would not only survive the next global famine—*it's coming*—but that you would stay safe and prosper; that you would find your Goshen and continue to grow in a Christian community. See my checklist for modern "Goshens" in this video: "The Safest Nations to Go if There's World War 3 | GOSHEN for Nomad Capitalists & Digital Nomads."

Going through a famine does not mean *you* are sinful! If you're living for God and face a famine, it means you live among *sinners* who will get judged from time to time. It's not your fault. Have faith to be protected during a famine.

PSALM 33:18-20

18 Behold, the eye of the Lord is on those who fear Him, On those who hope in His mercy,

19 To deliver their soul from death, And to keep them **alive in famine**.

20 Our soul waits for the Lord; He is our help and our shield.

. . .

FAMINE

PSALM 37:19

19 They shall not be ashamed in the evil time, And in the days of **famine** they shall be **satisfied**.

25 I have been young, and now am old; Yet I have **not** seen the righteous forsaken, Nor his descendants **begging bread**.

PROVERBS 10:3 The LORD will **not** allow the righteous soul to **famish**, But He casts away the desire of the wicked.

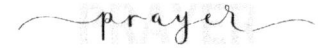

— prayer —

Revelation 6 warns us about the coming of the 4 Horsemen of the Apocalypse. The third horse—the **black horse**—is a prediction of global famine, which can refer to a global shortage or global depression. Preparing for such famines is a theme in the Bible.

GENESIS 41:54-55 The famine was in all lands, but in all the land of Egypt there was bread. **55** So when all the land of Egypt was famished, the people cried to Pharaoh for bread. Then Pharaoh said to all the Egyptians, "**Go to Joseph**; whatever he says to you, do."

COMMENT: Joseph settled his family in a specific region called **Goshen**. From this we get the concept of how to prepare for the next worldwide famine. The Lord will lead us to Goshens—places that will be relatively safe from a WW3 type scenario.

HOW / WHERE I'M PREPARING MY GOSHEN

_____

_____

_____

_____

_____

To join an international community of Christian "Preppers," subscribe to online church and download our private app at www.DiscoverChurch.Online

24
FAVOR

Tip: I am grateful for the immediate and lasting results of praying for God's unmerited favor. Truly God's favor is better than silver or gold (Proverbs 22:1). I challenge you to esteem God's favor more than your own individual efforts and see what God can accomplish in you and through you! Meditate on these Scriptures and ask God to apply His grace and favor to your life.

GENESIS 18:3 (the first instance of the word "favor") [Abraham] said, "My Lord, if I have now found **FAVOR** in Your sight, do not pass on by Your servant."

GENESIS 39:3-4 And his master saw that the LORD was with him and that the LORD made all he did to prosper in his hand. **4** So Joseph found **FAVOR** in his sight, and served him. Then he made him overseer of his house, and all that he had he put under his authority.

GENESIS 39:21 But the LORD was with Joseph [even in prison] and showed him mercy, and He gave him **FAVOR** in the sight of the keeper of the prison.

EXODUS 3:21 And I will give this people **FAVOR** in the sight of the Egyptians; and it shall be, when you go, that you shall not go empty-handed.

FAVOR

EXODUS 11:3 And the LORD gave the people **FAVOR** in the sight of the Egyptians. Moreover the man Moses was very great in the land of Egypt...

EXODUS 12:36 And the LORD had given the people **FAVOR** in the sight of the Egyptians, so that they granted them what they requested. Thus they plundered the Egyptians.

LEVITICUS 26:8-9 Five of you shall chase a hundred, and a hundred of you shall put ten thousand to flight; your enemies shall fall by the sword before you. **9** For I will look on you **FAVORABLY** and make you fruitful, multiply you and confirm My covenant with you.

1 SAMUEL 2:26 And the child Samuel grew in stature, and in **FAVOR** both with the LORD and men.

1 SAMUEL 16:22 Then Saul sent to Jesse, saying, "Please let David stand before me, for he has found **FAVOR** in my sight.

NEHEMIAH 2:5 And I said to the king, "If it pleases the king, and if your servant has found **FAVOR** in your sight, I ask that you send me to Judah, to the city of my fathers' tombs, that I may rebuild it."

ESTHER 2:9 Now the young woman pleased him [custodian], and she obtained his **FAVOR**... 2:15 And Esther obtained **FAVOR** in the sight of all who saw her. 2:17 The king loved Esther more than all the other women, and she obtained grace and **FAVOR** in his sight more than all the virgins; so he set the royal crown upon her head and made her queen instead of Vashti.

JOB 10:12 You have granted me life and **FAVOR** and Your care has preserved my spirit.

PSALM 5:12 For You, O LORD, will bless the righteous; with **FAVOR** You will surround him as with a shield.

PSALM 35:27 (AKJ) Let them shout for joy, and be glad, that **FAVOR** my righteous cause: yes, let them say continually, Let the LORD be magnified, which has pleasure in the prosperity of his servant.

PSALM 41:11 (AKJ) By this I know that you **FAVOR** me, because my enemy does not triumph over me.

PSALM 44:3 For they did not gain possession of the land by their own sword, Nor did their own arm save them; But it was Your right hand, Your arm, and the light of Your countenance, Because You **FAVOR** them.

PSALM 89:17 … in Your **FAVOR** our horn is exalted.

PSALM 118:58 I entreated Your **FAVOR** with my whole heart; be merciful to me according to Your word.

PROVERBS 3:3-4 Never let loyalty and kindness leave you! Tie them around your neck as a reminder. Write them deep within your heart. 4 Then you will find **FAVOR** with both God and people, and you will earn a good reputation.

PROVERBS 8:35 For whoever finds me [Wisdom] finds life, And obtains **FAVOR** from the LORD.

PROVERBS 12:2 A good man obtains **FAVOR** from the LORD….

PROVERBS 14:9 Fools mock at sin, But among the upright there is **FAVOR**.

PROVERBS 14:35 The king's **FAVOR** is toward a wise servant, But his wrath is against him who causes shame.

PROVERBS 16:15 (ESV) In the light of a king's face there is life, and his **FAVOR** is like clouds that brings the spring rain.

PROVERBS 18:22 He who finds a wife finds a good thing, And obtains **FAVOR** from the LORD. [See Proverbs 8:35]

PROVERBS 22:1 (ESV) A good name is to be chosen rather than great riches, and **FAVOR** is BETTER than silver or gold.

DANIEL 1:9 Now God had brought Daniel into the **FAVOR** and goodwill of the chief of the eunuchs.

(NIV) Now God had caused the official to show **FAVOR** and compassion to Daniel.

(ISV) God granted to Daniel **grace** and compassion on the part of the chief officer.

LUKE 1:30 Then the angel said to her, "Do not be afraid, Mary, for you have found **FAVOR** with God.

LUKE 2:52 And Jesus increased in wisdom and stature, and in **FAVOR** with God and men.

ACTS 2:46-47 So continuing daily with one accord in the temple, and breaking bread from house to house, they ate their food with gladness and simplicity of heart, **47** praising God and having **FAVOR** with all the people. And the Lord added to the church daily those who were being saved.

ACTS 7:9-10 And the patriarchs, becoming envious, sold Joseph into Egypt. But God was with him **10** and delivered him out of all his troubles, and gave him **FAVOR** and wisdom in the presence of Pharaoh, king of Egypt; and he made him governor over Egypt and all his house.

ACTS 7:46 [David] who found **FAVOR** before God and asked to find a dwelling for the God of Jacob. **47** But Solomon built Him a house. [Favor can pass down to your child or children.]

A Christian businessman approached me and asked for my help. He said he could not sell an empty piece of land he owned and it was not bringing him any income. He wanted to convert it to cash so he could build up his own farm. But no one would buy.

I asked him, "What Scriptures do you have when you pray?" He didn't have any and that's the reason he was asking for my help. So I told him, "When you need to sell something that's not selling, what you're really asking God for is not money but favor. His favor is worth more than money."

I asked him to read two Scriptures listed in this chapter: Proverbs 12:2 and Acts 2:47. I then asked him to pray based on what he read. He prayed the simplest prayer of faith a new believer could pray:

"Dear God, thank you for this pastor who showed me how to pray. He told me to read Acts 2:47, 'Praising God and having FAVOR with all the people.' I praise You, so my property has favor with all the people. This pastor also told me to read Proverbs 12:2, 'A good man obtains FAVOR from the LORD, But a man of wicked intentions He will condemn.' I ask You for favor to sell this property at a good price to a good person, not a wicked person. Let the buyer feel the presence of God on this property. Thank you for this pastor. I would have read these Scriptures without knowing how to use them. Now I get it. I pray and believe in Your Word, in Jesus' Name. Amen." His prayer was answered!

25
FUTURE

This is one of the most important prayers I prayed for a decade before I stepped into my destiny and a greater prophetic anointing.

ASK ME ABOUT YOUR FUTURE

JEREMIAH 29:11-13 "For I know the plans I have for you," declares the LORD, "plans to prosper you and not to harm you, plans to give you hope and a future. **12** Then you will call upon me and come and pray to me, and I will listen to you. **13** You will seek me and find me when you seek me with all your heart.

ISAIAH 45:11 …Ask Me of things to come concerning My sons; And concerning the work of My hands, you command Me.

GOD WANTS ME TO KNOW WHAT HE KNOWS

1 CORINTHIANS 12:1 Now concerning spiritual gifts, brethren, I do **not** want you to be **ignorant**.

ROMANS 11:25 For I do **not** desire, brethren, that you should be **ignorant** of this mystery…

1 THESSALONIANS 4:13 But I do **not** want you to be **ignorant**, brethren, concerning those who have fallen asleep, lest you sorrow as others who have no hope.

HOLY SPIRIT SHOW ME!

ROMANS 8:26-27 Likewise the Spirit also helps in our weaknesses. For we do not know what we should pray for as we ought, but the Spirit Himself makes intercession for us with groanings which cannot be uttered. **27** Now He who searches the hearts knows what the **mind of the Spirit** is, because He makes intercession for the saints according to the will of God.

JOHN 14:26 But the Helper, the Holy Spirit, whom the Father will send in My name, He will **teach you all things**, and bring to your remembrance all things that I said to you.

JOHN 16:13 However, when He, the Spirit of truth, has come, He will **guide you** into all truth; for He will not speak on His own authority, but whatever He hears He will speak; and He will **tell you things to come**.

PROVERBS 16:9 A man's heart plans his way, But the LORD directs his steps.

ZECHARIAH 4:6... Not by might nor by power, but by My Spirit,' says the LORD of hosts.

FIVE TIMELESS KEYS YOU'VE GIVEN ME

1. **God has a PLAN for my life.** I seek Him [pray] to understand and fulfill His plans.
2. **God does NOT want me to be ignorant**, but to be informed about spiritual truths and the future.
3. **The Holy Spirit will TEACH me ALL things**; there are no limitations to the subject or request! I can learn anything.
4. **The Holy Spirit will GUIDE me into ALL truth**; in things I don't know how to do or when to do, I am not clueless or helpless. I have a Guide inside!
5. **Success in family, friendships, ministry, business, investments is not by might, nor by power, but by the SPIRIT.** I know what to do by the peace of God (Isaiah 55:12).

I am Spirit-filled, so I am peace-filled. There is no fear in God's leading. There is absolutely nothing to fear or worry over.

COLOSSIANS 4:12 Epaphras, who is one of you… always laboring fervently for you in prayers, that you may stand perfect and complete in all the will of God.

PRAY: *My prayer, Father, is that I, my family and our entire church may stand perfect and complete in all the will of God. My desire is to always be in the center of Your perfect will.*

Holy Spirit, I pray that You take the lead. Please cultivate Your relationship with me and bring me to the place where You can totally trust me and entrust great wealth & influence to me. You are setting me up; all things work for my good. Please do exceedingly abundantly above all I ask or think (Ephesians 3:20).

THINGS MY FATHER WANTS TO SHOW ME

PRAY: *Lord, You have the plans for my life. By faith, I ask You in Jesus' Name to reveal everything I need to know to love You, serve You and be a success in Your eyes.*

I believe I hear Your will, the timing of Your will, and how to fulfill Your will step-by-step. I confess success each day for myself, our family, friends, church and ministry!

You said You are my Guide. I believe You are guiding me. You said You would teach me ALL things, so I set no limit as to what You will teach me:

- Show me how to win more souls, impact more lives, influence more leaders, and multiply more disciples across the world through more channels.
- Show me how to love my wife and train our children so they will always love and serve You, follow Your call, obey Your commands, and stay loyal to us as parents.
- Show me how to be a better friend, enjoy Your gifts, be more grateful and have more fun in life. Show me how to walk in divine health all the time.
- Show me how to pastor people the way Jesus would, so Discover Church will grow deep, grow strong, and grow healthy.

- Show me how to operate a global ministry, build up ministry partners, and treat our supporters.
- Show me how to allocate my assets at the right time in the right places at the right proportion in the right way through the right people or organizations.
- Show me which investments are best to buy and sell, and when to enter and exit.
- Show me where are the best real estate properties to buy, rent and sell, and when to move.
- Show me ministry and business opportunities that are uncommon, non-time consuming, and highly rewarding.

Would You invite me to minister to the best people, at the best churches in the world? Let us network with good people and be part of the most anointed events.

Would You put holy desires in me? For all things desirable are possible! (Mark 9:23) You give me the desires of my heart. (Psalm 37:4)

Would You grant me more gifts of the Spirit? 3 out of 9 gifts are about revelation, so You want me to have not only clear but supernatural direction through the word of wisdom, word of knowledge, and discerning of spirits. I welcome the fullness of the gifts of the Holy Spirit. I humbly ask and believe I receive by grace more supernatural visitations, leadings, words in seasons, keen insights, practical wisdom and ears to hear the voice of God.

Would You grant us more outpourings of the Spirit, a burden for prayer, sensitivity to Your will, a tender heart to change, and boldness to obey? May all of us prophesy, see visions and dream dreams. Expand us, enlarge our tents, multiply our resources, for the glory of God. Rearrange our lives, Lord, to fit Your will.

COLOSSIANS 1:9 ...we have not stopped praying for you and asking God to fill you with the knowledge of his will through all spiritual wisdom and understanding.

FUTURE DIRECTIONS

_____

_____

_____

26
GOALS & PRIORITIES

Written dreams become measurable goals. Goals that we do not commit to paper are simply wishes. They don't have weight in the spirit realm.

Goal-setting and dream board-making have become popular ways to exercise one's faith. My family and I have found them to be effective. Each year our children select photos and cut out images that represent their dreams. It's amazing how they come to pass.

One year my son Austin put on his dream board that he wished he had a brother. My wife and I had no intention of having another child, but we didn't quench his dream board. We let him express his faith and left it with God to answer him.

Two years later, one of my spiritual sons had his firstborn and the child came out looking exactly like the boy on Austin's dream board! We were amazed at how God honored his faith put on paper. We couldn't imagine God would do it that way. Austin loves little David.

Here were my 16 written goals in 1999. Some of them are not be quantifiable, but they are personally meaningful to me.

GOALS & PRIORITIES

prayer

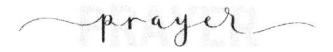

1. To be known as a person of love. Christ's greatest commandments are to love God and to love people.

MATTHEW 22:37-40 (KJV) Thou shalt love the Lord with all thy heart, and with all thy soul, and with all thy mind. This is the first and great commandment. And the second is like unto it, Thou shalt love thy neighbor as thyself. On these two commandments hang all the law and the prophets.

All the joy and fulfillment I desire in this life come from these two relationships: one with God and one with others.

EPHESIANS 3:19 (NASB95) and to know the love of Christ which surpasses knowledge…

How can I "know" something that "surpasses knowledge"? In the natural, it's an impossibility. It takes a supernatural revelation to "know" the "unknowable" love of Christ. I want to know God's love.

JOHN 5:12 (KJV) This is my commandment, That ye love one another, as I have loved you. Greater love hath no man than this, that a man lay down his life for his friends.

The distinguishing characteristic of men and women greatly used of God is that they loved.

2. To put total trust in God. Total trust throws away everything that hints at self-promotion or impatience; to guard above all things my heart (my motives), instead of trying to guard my interests. Faith doesn't last in a self-centered or impatient heart. I will not promote myself. I will not rush.

PROVERBS 19:2 …he that hasteth with his feet sinneth.

ISAIAH 28:16 …he that believeth shall not make haste.

I will guard my motives. If I think I may do anything for advantage sake or for self-promotion sake, I will intentionally stop and trust God to open doors, invite me to minister, and trust Him to confirm His will to me in prayer.

3. To highly esteem the value of relationships God has given me. It is better to have no money, no luxury, no travel, no big house, no big ministry, but have a big, happy relationship. It is priceless.

4. To put character above gifts. To transform my personality by beholding God's Word and God's Glory (Romans 12:2, 2 Corinthians 3:18).

I aim to consistently produce in my life the fruit of the Spirit. I am more loving, more joyful, more peaceful, more long-suffering, more gentle, more good, more faithful, more meek, and more temperate. (Galatians 5:22-23) What does each fruit mean?

> **Love** = be vulnerable. Allow and accept differences. Make it safe for others to disagree with me.
> **Joy** = be positive. Enjoy life, be playful, have fun, be funny.
> **Peace** = be quiet. Pursue peace! No strife! Proverbs 15:1 says, *A mild reply turns wrath aside; but a sharp word will stir up anger.* Proverbs 16:32, *A forbearing man is better than a fighting man; he who controls himself is better than a conqueror.* Proverbs 19:11, *The discretion of a man deferreth his anger; and it is his glory to pass over a transgression. A man's prudence will make him slow to take offense; to pass over an offense is his glory.*
> **Long-suffering or Patience** = be patient, be slow, be flexible. Until sure, don't move. God can repeat Himself and confirm His will. Don't be stubborn. Learn to compromise on non-essentials.
> **Gentleness** = be soft. Don't insist on my own ways. Never lose my temper. Hold hands. Hug. Cry.
> **Goodness** = be friendly. Give gifts. Proverbs 19:6 says, *Every man is a friend to him that giveth gifts.* Be quick to appreciate, slow to judge. Don't be critical or listen to gossip. Proverbs 16:21, *A wise man is esteemed for being pleasant; his friendly words add to his influence.*
> **Faith** = be genuine. Faith works by my words. Do my words have weight? The test of faith is a test of genuineness. Am I true? Is there any lie in me? Get rid of fakery.
> **Meekness** = Be humble. Appreciate others first. Find something to thank before talking or writing. Be grateful. Not obsequious or seeking other's approval. Proverbs 18:12…*before honor is humility.* As far as other humans go, I expect nothing and I appreciate everything.
> **Temperance or Self-Control** = be moderate. Be temperate. Have self-control. Don't be dogmatic. Try to see others' perspectives.

Notice that some of the fruits of the spirit begin to sound alike. Why is that? Because they are different manifestations of the same fruit. That's why the "fruit" is singular even though there are nine facets.

It's possible that when you have more of one, you feel as though you have less of the other. For instance, if you had more humility, you might need less long-suffering. If you exercised faith boldly, you may seem to be less gentle.

5. To seek wisdom above all from God's Word. I chose to improve. Read the Bible every day. (Proverbs 4:20-22.)

6. To tithe my time every day except Sunday. I have had good examples to learn from: godly men who pray a lot. Start the day by putting Him first. (Matthew 6:33.)

7. To not take money from people with questionable motives. Don't accept "donations" with strings attached. I will not depend financially on my parents; I will be a blessing to them.

8. To ask more questions. (See the next chapter.) Spend time with wise people and listen to their wisdom.

9. To talk less. Don't respond out of impulse. Be slow to speak.

PROVERBS 15:28 A good man ponders what to say: bad men let out a flood of evil talk.

PROVERBS 16:23 Good sense makes men judicious in their talk...

PROVERBS 17:27 A man of sense is sparing of his words; the prudent will keep cool.

PROVERBS 17:27-28 He that hath knowledge spareth his words: and a man of understanding is of an excellent spirit. Even a fool, when he holdeth his peace, is counted wise: and he that shutteth his lips is esteemed a man of understanding.

PROVERBS 21:23 He who is careful of his lips and tongue will manage to keep clear of trouble.

PROVERBS 30:32 If thou hast done foolishly in lifting up thyself, or if thou hast thought evil, lay thine hand upon thy mouth.

10. To learn to take myself lightly.

I take God seriously, but I don't take myself too seriously because (a) I'm not indispensable, (b) I'm replaceable, (c) the smartest people I know are funny. (Matthew 22:8-9 [the Wedding Banquet, where guests were replaced], 1 Corinthians 12:26 [we are One Body, and members of one another], 1 Corinthians 9:27 [Paul said if he doesn't keep his body in check, he could be a castaway], Philippians 3:12-14 [Paul said he had not already attained, he is pressing toward the mark for the prize].)

11. Win 100 people to Christ each year. (1 Timothy 2:4, 2 Peter 3:9, Psalm 2:8, Isaiah 11:9, Habakkuk 2:14, Matthew 24:40.)

12. Have a tent-making business that generates residual income and helps the ministry. (Acts 18:3 [Paul and Aquila were tentmakers], 2 Thessalonians 3:10.)

13. Have a million dollars in investments that grow 10-30% per year. (Luke 19:16, 18, 23.)

14. Buy a house for my parents within a decade. (Mark 7:10-12 [Honor your parents means honor them financially], Proverbs 3:9 [Honor with substance, not merely words].)

15. Keep learning to be more relatable to people and more effective in ministry. Help people know how important they are to God and how I love them. Psalm 119:97-100 says, *Thou through thy commandments hast made me WISER than mine enemies: for they are ever with me. I have MORE understanding than all my teachers: for thy testimonies are my meditation. I understand MORE than the ancients, because I keep thy precepts.*

16. To become a statesman in the Body of Christ. To be a leader to leaders. Samuel and Nathan were leaders to David. Paul "the aged" was a leader to Timothy, Titus, and Philemon (1:9). Once I pass 50, I will walk as a statesman for the Lord.

GOALS & PRIORITIES

7 PRIORITIES

FAITH:
_____
_____
_____
_____
_____

FITNESS:
_____
_____
_____
_____
_____

FAMILY:
_____
_____
_____
_____
_____

FINANCES:
_____
_____

FRIENDS:

FUN:

FOOD / FASTING:

GOALS & PRIORITIES

Wise aphorisms that motivate me to achieve my goals:

- Feelings follow thoughts and actions.
- Knowledge of weakness is the first step towards growth.
- We should all wear a sign that says *Under Construction*.
- Watch out about getting in a hurry in business or in ministry. If you're in a hurry, you'll miss God.
- Those who *wait* upon the Lord shall renew their strength and fly like eagles. (Isaiah 40:31)
- We really can't *enjoy* life until we learn how to see and say something positive about everything.
- It's easy to be depressed: just think about yourself all the time.
- Pride is self-righteous, self-centered and self-absorbed; it's great freedom when you can go for hours and days at a time not thinking about yourself.
- Put God first and think about others.

27
GRACE

Grace is God's unmerited favor. It's being blessed something you didn't earn or deserve. God gives grace to the humble. While it's not Scriptural to ask God for more faith (it's your decision to trust someone based on how well you know them), it's perfectly Scriptural to ask God for more grace. The act of asking is a sign of your humility.

JAMES 4:6 (KJV) But he giveth MORE GRACE. Wherefore he saith, God resisteth the proud, but giveth GRACE unto the humble.

1 PETER 5:5 (KJV) Likewise, ye longer, submit yourselves unto the elder. Yea, all of you be subject one to another, and be clothed with humility: for God resisteth the proud, but giveth GRACE to the humble.

ZECHARIAH 12:10 And I will pour upon the house of David, and upon the inhabitants of Jerusalem, the spirit of GRACE and of supplications [TLB says "prayer"]: and they shall look upon me whom they have pierced, and they shall mourn for him, as one mourneth for his only son, and shall be in bitterness for him, as one that is in bitterness for his firstborn.

HEBREWS 4:15-16 (KJV) For we have not an high priest [Jesus] which cannot be touched with the feeling of our infirmities [weaknesses]; but was in all points tempted like as we are, yet without sin. **16** Let us therefore come BOLDLY unto the throne of GRACE, that we may obtain mercy and find GRACE to help in time of need.

GRACE

ACTS 14:3 (KJV) Long time therefore abode they speaking boldly in the Lord, which gave testimony unto the WORD of his GRACE, and granted signs and wonders to be done by their hands.

ACTS 20:32 And now, brethren, I commend you to God, and to the WORD of his GRACE, which is able to build you up, and to give you an inheritance among all them which are sanctified.

COMMENT: This was Paul's farewell blessing to the church elders he raised up in the present day Turkish city of Ephesus. For many years I made this my personal blessing when I prayed over others. I pray it in the Good News version:

> *"And now I commend you to the care of God and to the message of his grace, which is able to build you up and give you the blessings God has for all his people."*

ACTS 4:33 And with great power gave the apostles witness of the resurrection of the Lord Jesus: and GREAT **GRACE** was upon them all.

PRAY: *"Lord, give me great grace so I can be a powerful witness for Jesus wherever I go."*

TITUS 2:11-13 (KJV) For the **GRACE** of God that bringeth salvation hath appeared to all men, **12** Teaching us that, denying ungodliness and worldly lusts, we should live soberly, righteously, and godly, in this present world; **13** Looking for that blessed hope, and the glorious appearing of the great God and our Saviour Jesus Christ;

COMMENT: According to Paul, grace not only saves us, it also teaches us. If our belief in God's grace doesn't instruct us, it's not grace—it's human permissiveness.

Grace *teaches* saved people to become better Christians who deny ungodliness and worldly lusts. Grace *teaches* us to live soberly. Grace *instructs* us to pay attention to Bible prophecy and take the end times seriously. Any "grace teaching" that is all about my forgiveness, my blessing, my security in Christ—any grace teaching that does not lead to living right and getting ready for the Day of Judgment, is a misrepresentation of Biblical grace.

GET PRAYERS ANSWERED

Things that came by GRACE for me

_____
_____
_____
_____
_____
_____
_____
_____
_____
_____
_____
_____
_____
_____
_____
_____
_____
_____
_____
_____

If you are looking for how to "say grace" over a meal, see the chapter "Eating." A related chapter is to encourage you is "Favor."

28
HEALING

5 Healing Steps

Here is a prescription for your healing. When you go to the doctor's office, you may get a prescription. You may be unsure if it will work, but you—by faith—follow it. In a similar way, follow God's instructions for your healing. The Gospel of Luke tells us twice that sick people came "to hear and to be healed" by Jesus (Luke 5:15, 6:17). If only your praying matters, and hearing Biblical instructions doesn't matter, why would Luke the Physician record they had to first "hear" and then they were "healed"?

1. Take God's Medicine.

PROVERBS 4:20-22

20 My son, give attention to my words; Incline your ear to my sayings.

21 Do not let them depart from your eyes; Keep them in the midst of your heart;

22 For they are life to those who find them, And health [or medicine] to all their flesh.

God's Word is God's Medicine. When you're weak or sick, double up on your daily medicine! If you read 2 chapters of the Bible a day, then read 4 a day when you're trying to get strong. Read 10 to get stronger. People have been healed by doing nothing more than taking more of God's medicine!

MATTHEW 4:4 …'Man shall not live by bread alone, but by every word that proceeds from the mouth of God.'

MATTHEW 6:11 Give us this day our daily bread.

Another way to double up on God's medicine is to read Christian books on the subject of healing. Pay attention to **audios and videos on healing**. Some well-intentioned people may give you reading and watching materials that have nothing to do with healing. Put those on the shelf. Focus. *"My son and daughter, give attention to MY WORDS."*

If you want to be healed, put healing thoughts, words, stories, and examples into your spirit. Isn't it true "what you put in is what you get out"?

Another great way to fill up on healing is to attend a church that believes and trains people in divine healing. Many people in our church have been healed before anyone ever prayed for them. How? By sitting under the anointed preaching of God's Word.

I believe that's how those sick people got healed in Luke 5:15 and 6:17. There's no indication Jesus ever laid hands on them. They listened attentively and their disease disappeared! God did that for them—why not for you, too?

ISAIAH 32:3 The **eyes** of those who see will not be dim, and the **ears** of those who hear will listen. **4** Also the **heart** of the rash will understand knowledge, and the **tongue** of the stammerers will be ready to speak plainly.

You're never too old to get better.

DEUTERONOMY 34:7 And Moses was an hundred and twenty years old when he died: his eye was not dim, nor his natural force abated.

He still had his strength, health and vitality. Moses climbed up a mountain and passed away in peace at 120. No one helped him up a mountain. You don't have to be sick to go to Heaven!

2. Speak Words of Life.

Speak what you want [healing], not what you fear [pain or dying]. You must decide what kind of words you speak when sick. Faith words turn hopeless situations around. Faith is not denying reality, but changing reality. Yes, the doctor may say they have reached the limits of medical science to help you, but with God nothing shall be impossible.

PROVERBS 18:21 Death and life are in the power of the tongue, And those who love it will eat its fruit.

Words are free. It's just as easy to say words of doubt as it is to say words of faith. It does not matter if you don't "feel like" speaking positively. Faith in your heart will work with doubt in your head, because faith works by words, not by feelings.

JAMES 3:10 Out of the same mouth proceed blessing and cursing. My brethren, these things ought not to be so.

By faith, speak God's Word about healing and healing will flow.

ISAIAH 33:24 And the inhabitant will not say, "I am sick"; The people who dwell in it will be forgiven their iniquity.

CONFESS: *I receive the DOUBLE BLESSING of Isaiah 33—healing and forgiveness. Redemption means I'm doubly blessed because of Jesus—in Christ I'm forgiven and healed.*

MATTHEW 8:17 …He Himself took our infirmities and bore our sicknesses.

SAY: *I believe Jesus Himself took my _____ [name your disease] and bore my _____ [name your symptoms].*

1 PETER 2:24 [Jesus] Himself bore our sins in His own body on the tree [cross], that we, having died to sins, might live for righteousness—by whose stripes you were healed.

SAY: *God's Word says I was already healed. I'm not going to be healed, because I was! I'm not waiting for God to do something, God has already done it for me! I agree with 1 Peter 2:24, I refuse to take sides against God's Word. Jesus paid for the price of sin and sickness, it's up to me to believe and receive His Word. Thank You Lord for making Jesus my Doctor and Healer. Hallelujah!*

Don't doubt the power of anointed words.

. . .

MARK 11:22-24

22 So Jesus answered and said to them, "Have faith in God.

23 For assuredly, I say to you, whoever says to this mountain, 'Be removed and be cast into the sea,' and does not doubt in his heart, but believes that those things he says will be done, he will have whatever he says.

24 Therefore I say to you, whatever things you ask when you pray, believe that you receive them, and you will have them.

Faith does not mean quitting your medicine or not having an operation. Faith has to do with the words you choose to speak. You can avoid an operation out of fear and you wouldn't be any more in faith. When you are in faith, trusting God, you have peace in your heart no matter what you do.

3. WALK IN LOVE

The number one reason Christians are sick is NOT because they don't have enough faith or that they are living in some gross sin. The number one reason Christians are defeated is that they walk out of love.

Get back in love. Make a decision to forgive and refuse to hold grudges, take vengeance or be vindictive. Suffering injustice does not authorize us to retaliate; it will only hurt our faith.

GALATIANS 5:6 (KJV) …faith worketh by love.

Faith works by love and love works by faith. The two are inseparable.

EXODUS 15:26 and God said, "If you diligently heed the voice of the Lord your God and do what is right in His sight, give ear to His commandments and keep all His statutes, I will put none of the diseases on you which I have brought on the Egyptians. For I am the Lord who heals you."

All of God's commandments under the old covenant were summarized by Jesus in one word: LOVE. If we love, we fulfill God's commands, and when we do, we can expect God to be our "Jehovah-Rapha" ~ the Lord our Healer. Until then, we are only hoping to be healed, but we cannot be confident that we are indeed healed.

MARK 12:30-31 And you shall love the Lord your God with all your heart, with all your soul, with all your mind, and with all your strength.' This is the first commandment. **31** And the second, like it, is this: 'You shall love your neighbor as yourself.' There is no other commandment greater than these."

Love is the fulfilling of the law. Love is God's will. It's important that we know we are in God's will BEFORE we pray, otherwise our hearts will condemn us and we will not approach God confidently.

1 JOHN 3:21-22 Beloved, if our heart does not condemn us, we have confidence toward God. **22** And whatever we ask we receive from Him, because we keep His commandments and do those things that are pleasing in His sight.

If you have offended anyone, humble yourself and ask them for forgiveness. If anyone has offended you, don't get even. Don't do what you know will hurt them. Show mercy. Show kindness. If they are gone or out of your life, release them with your words, "I forgive [name the person]. I let them go. Lord, bless them and show Your goodness to them." You don't have to "feel" like forgiving, you just have to make a quality decision and stick with it. Feelings follow faith and action!

Now be assured you are in God's will! According to the Bible, it is His will that your prayer be answered, your body be healed and your mind be whole - Hallelujah!

1 JOHN 5:14-15 Now this is the confidence that we have in Him, that if we ask anything according to His will, He hears us. **15** And if we know that He hears us, whatever we ask, we know that we have the petitions that we have asked of Him.

4. RESIST WORRY

After having followed God's instruction – read the Bible every day and go to a church that teaches uncompromisingly about healing. Change your words to agree with God's Word, even before you see or feel any physical changes. Make a choice to walk in love towards everyone in your life, bless and do not curse, do good for them. Now refuse to worry.

Worry is the thief of God's blessings.

PHILIPPIANS 4:6 (NET) Do not be anxious [worry, fret or be afraid] about anything. Instead, in every situation, through prayer and petition with thanksgiving, tell your requests to God.

1 PETER 5:7 (KJV) Casting all your care [worry] upon him; for he careth for you.

MATTHEW 6:25, 31-33 (NET)

25 "Therefore I tell you, do not worry about your life, what you will eat or drink, or about your body, what you will wear. Isn't there more to life than food and more to the body than clothing?...

31 So then, don't worry saying, 'What will we eat?' or 'What will we drink?' or 'What will we wear?'

32 For the unconverted pursue these things, and your heavenly Father knows that you need them.

33 But above all pursue his kingdom and righteousness, and all these things will be given to you as well.

We worry because we doubt God will come through for us. Worry leads to depression. Worry is absolutely useless. Worry is a sin. Most people think of sin as something outward, like murder and adultery, but God views sins of the heart as seriously as sins of the flesh, perhaps even more! Jealousy is a form of worry. Greed is a form of worry. Losing sleep and not eating right are expressions of worry. Make the decision not to fall into worry.

Worry is believing the worst will happen to you, despite God's Word promising the opposite!

ROMANS 8:28 And we know that all things work together for good to those who love God, to those who are the called according to His purpose.

Resist worry by telling God, "Lord, I cast all my worries and cares upon You, because I know You care for me. You are watching over me. All things are working together for my good because I love You and am called according to Your purpose. I can live worry free and sickness free, in Jesus' Name. Amen."

5. ACCEPT JESUS AS YOUR SAVIOR & HEALER

I find that when people are sick, they often reassess their lives. They tend to think about what is important versus frivolous. Others around them may get uncomfortable with this, but I believe it is a healthy process. God is very comfortable with you assessing your life. God has been, in fact, waiting for you to be honest about your mistakes and come clean with your sins, then turn to Christ. This is a good place to be.

Surrender your life now to Christ. He alone can clean up your mess, wash away your past, and give you a new start. He died on the Cross as your substitute. He defeated death and hell and rose again from the dead after three days. He is alive and coming back to judge the living and the dead. As wonderful as physical healing is, nothing compares to eternal salvation. When we are healed, we only live a few more years on earth. But when we are saved by the Blood of Jesus, we get to live in Heaven forever and ever.

ROMANS 10:9, 11 that if you confess with your mouth the Lord Jesus and believe in your heart that God has raised Him from the dead, you will be saved... **11** For the Scripture says, "Whoever believes on Him will not be put to shame."

PRAY NOW: *I believe Jesus is truly the Son of God and the sinless Savior of the world. Thank You for dying on the Cross as my substitute. Thank You for paying the penalty of all my sins, too many to count. I believe You defeated death, hell and the grave, so I have no more fear of dying. You are my God, my Savior, my Healer. I am saved and I am healed. From this day onwards, my life is Yours. Help me find a good church, live for Your purpose and serve You till I see You face-to-face. In Jesus' Name I pray. Amen.*

Keep feeding on healing. Believe God wants you well. Remember you don't have to die from sickness, any more than someone must die by accident. (See chapter "Aging.") People get what they believe and say. Say what the Word says. You can get healed at any age, live a full life for God, and when you're ready, go meet Your Creator and Redeemer in peace.

INSTANCES OF GOD HEALING ME

_____

_____

_____

_____

Glorify God by sharing your story of healing: www.discover.org.au

29
HOME DEDICATION

Before moving in, a house should be cleansed and dedicated to the Lord. We call this the "house cleansing" and "home blessing."

DECLARE: *The Word of God is the foundation of our home and protects our family's future.*

ACTION: *When I build a new house, I have the opportunity to put God's Word into its foundation. I do a prophetic act by printing and laminating these Scriptures and placing them right in the concrete foundation or under a wooden deck.*

HOUSE CLEANSING

LUKE 10:5-7 But whatever HOUSE you enter, first say, 'PEACE to this HOUSE.' **6** And if a son of peace is there, your peace will rest on it; if not, it will return to you. **7** And remain in the same house, eating and drinking such things as they give, for the laborer is worthy of his wages. Do not go from house to house.

MARK 6:10,12-13 Also He said to them, "In whatever place you enter a HOUSE, stay there till you depart from that place.... **12** So they went out and preached that people should repent. **13** And they CAST OUT many demons, and anointed with oil many who were sick, and healed them"

HOME DEDICATION

HOME BLESSING

JOSHUA 1:3 "Every place that the sole of your foot will tread upon I have given you, as I said to Moses"

JOSHUA 24:15 But as for me and my HOUSE, we will serve the LORD.

ISAIAH 32:18 My people will live in peaceful dwelling places, in secure homes, in undisturbed places of rest.

PSALM 122:7 "PEACE be within your walls, PROSPERITY within your palaces"

PSALM 127:1-4 (KJV)

1 Except the LORD build the house, they labour in vain that build it: except the LORD keep the city, the watchman waketh but in vain.

2 It is vain for you to rise up early, to sit up late, to eat the bread of sorrows: for so he giveth his beloved sleep.

3 Lo, children are an heritage of the LORD: and the fruit of the womb is his reward.

4 As arrows are in the hand of a mighty man; so are children of the youth.

5 Happy is the man that hath his quiver full of them: they shall not be ashamed, but they shall speak with the enemies in the gate.

PSALM 121:7-8 "The Lord shall preserve you from all evil; He shall preserve your soul. The Lord shall preserve your going OUT and your coming IN. From this time forth, and even forevermore"

1 CORINTHIANS 3:11 For no man can lay a foundation other than the one which is laid, which is Jesus Christ.

BLESSINGS ON THE FAMILY

DEUTERONOMY 28:3-8 "Blessed shall you be in the CITY, and blessed shall you be in the COUNTRY. **4** Blessed shall be the fruit of your body, the produce of your ground and the increase of your herds, the increase of your cattle and the offspring of your flocks. **5** Blessed shall be your basket and your kneading bowl. **6** Blessed shall you be when you COME IN, and blessed shall you be when you GO OUT. **7** The Lord will cause your ENEMIES who rise against you to be defeated before your face; they shall come out against you one way and FLEE before you seven ways. **8** The Lord will command the blessing on you in your STOREHOUSES and in all to which you set your hand, and He will bless you in the LAND which the Lord your God is giving you."

ISAIAH 8:18 Behold, I and the CHILDREN whom the LORD hath given me are for signs and for wonders in Israel from the LORD of hosts, which dwelleth in mount Zion.

PSALM 112:1-4 (ESV)

1 Praise the LORD! Blessed is the man who fears the LORD, who greatly delights in his commandments!

2 His OFFSPRING will be mighty in the land; the generation of the upright will be blessed.

3 Wealth and riches are in his HOUSE, and his righteousness endures forever.

4 Light dawns in the darkness for the upright; he is gracious, merciful, and righteous.

PSALM 37:23-29

23 The steps of a good man are ordered by the Lord, And He delights in his way

25 I have been young, and now am old; Yet I have not seen the righteous forsaken, Nor his DESCENDANTS begging bread.

26 He is ever merciful, and lends; And his DESCENDANTS are blessed.

28 For the Lord loves justice, And does not forsake His saints; They are preserved forever, But the descendants of the wicked shall be cut off.

29 The righteous shall inherit the LAND, And dwell in it forever.

HOME DEDICATION

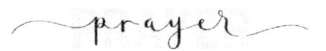

prayer

PSALM 91:1-16 (God's Word)

1 Whoever lives under the SHELTER of the Most High will remain in the shadow of the Almighty.

5 You do not need to fear terrors of the night, arrows that fly during the day,

6 plagues that roam the dark, epidemics that strike at noon.

7 They will not come near you, even though a thousand may fall dead beside you or ten thousand at your right side.

10 No harm will come to you. No sickness will come near your HOUSE.

11 He will put his angels in charge of you to protect you in all your ways.

This is how I would cleanse and bless a home before moving in. You can call on your pastor to bless your home. Some ministers will anoint the home with oil.

30
HOUSES TO THE GODLY

Tip: Everybody needs a house to live in, especially if they are a newly married couple. God commands them to leave their father and mother, so it's assumed they have their own home. The Bible promises not only a house for you, but houses (plural). It is a godly thing to rely on God for a house, rather than pay rent to make someone else rich or rely on someone else to take care of you.

When my mother needed a house, I found these Scriptures for her and prayed the prayer of agreement with her based on these promises. God gave her the house she wanted. It has been a house of prayer and a place of blessing for others. Several people in my church have also applied these Scriptures and received their own houses. Trust the Lord to make good His Word!

ADDRESS OF THE HOUSE I'M PRAYING FOR

_____

_____

_____

prayer

EXODUS 1:21 And it came to pass, because the midwives feared God, that he made them HOUSES.

DEUTERONOMY 6:10-11 (KJV)

10 And it shall be, when the LORD thy God shall have brought thee into the land which he sware unto thy fathers, to Abraham, to Isaac, and to Jacob, to GIVE THEE great and godly cities, which thou buildedst not,

11 And HOUSES full of all good things, which thou filledst not, and wells digged, which thou diggedst not, vineyards and olive trees, which thou plantedst not; when thou shalt have eaten and be full;

LEVITICUS 25:33 And if a man purchase of the Levites, then the house that was sold, and the city of his possession, shall go out in the year of jubilee: for the HOUSES of the cities of the Levites are their POSSESSION among the children of Israel.

ISAIAH 65:21-22 And they shall BUILD HOUSES, and inhabit them; and they shall plant vineyards, and eat the fruit of them. **22** They shall not build, and another inhabit; they shall not plant, and another eat: for as the days of a tree are the days of my people, and mine elect shall long enjoy the work of their hands.

MARK 10:29-31 And Jesus answered and said, Verily I say unto you, There is no man that hath left house, or brethren, or sisters, or father, or mother, or wife, or children, or lands, for my sake, and the gospel's, **30** But he shall receive an hundredfold NOW in this time, HOUSES, and brethren, and sisters, and mothers, and children, and lands, with persecutions; and in the world to come eternal life. **31** But many that are first shall be last; and the last first.

1 CORINTHIANS 11:22 (KJV) What? have ye not HOUSES to eat and to drink in? ... [Answer: Yes, we do!]

DEUTERONOMY 11:23-25

23 Then will the LORD drive out all these nations from before you, and ye shall possess greater nations and mightier than yourselves.

24 EVERY PLACE whereon the soles of your feet shall tread SHALL BE YOURS: from the wilderness and Lebanon, from the river, the river Euphrates, even unto the uttermost sea shall your coast be.

25 There shall no man be able to stand before you: for the LORD your God shall lay the fear of you and the dread of you upon ALL THE LAND that ye shall tread upon, as he hath said unto you.

QUALITIES & LOCATION OF MY DREAM HOME

_____
_____
_____
_____
_____
_____
_____
_____
_____
_____

A related chapter is "Church Property." In the process of taking care of God's House, I was blessed with various homes over the years.

31

HUSBAND

This is the only prayer in my guidebook for which I didn't directly receive an answer. I've only prayed for my wife, who says my prayers have helped her. So in the interest of being fair, I offer some thoughts on how to pray for your husbands.

(Men, you can pray this for yourselves to be the type of leader who will not miss the will of God or bring pain to the lives of wives and children.)

First, if you're a single lady, you should only choose to marry a Christian man who shares your interests *and* your energy level (Second Corinthians 6:14). Most women I know aspire to marry someone successful and rich, but they don't realize that if their energy levels are incompatible, the marriage will likely fall apart.

This is the simplest explanation for why no woman can stay married to **Elon Musk.** He is the world's richest man. Countless women dream of living with the world's richest man. After 3 failed marriages and 12 children with 3 different women (one of whom he was not married to), Elon no longer has wives. Why? No one can keep up with a man who runs Tesla, Starlink, Neural Link, Space X, X Corp (formerly Twitter) and xAI simultaneously.

It's not to say it's impossible to be married to a rich man, but the energy levels have to be similar. **Donald Trump** has been married 3 times—every time to a model: a Czech model, Miss Hawaii USA, and a Slovenian model. Only Melania seems to be able to keep up with him.

Donald Trump sleeps only 4 hours a day. He built an international real estate organization, luxury hotels, golf courses, starred in his own hit TV show, founded his own university (now closed), campaigned tirelessly from state to state to be President of the United States, fought unjust court battles, started his own social media company, and was shot in the ear during his 2024 bid for the US Presidency. Not many women can be happy with that.

Is he successful? Yes, he's still among the Fortune 500 richest people on earth. Many women would love to be married to one of the Fortune 500 men. But they don't think about their incompatibility. To be someone's lifelong partner, you should at least make his life easier. You should make his life better.

If you as a woman have low energy and the man you admire has high energy, it is unlikely that the two of you will be compatible. My advice is pick someone comparable to you. Don't make life more difficult for someone else.

It is simply easier to pick a compatible man than to pray for the wrong man. The "right" man should not be someone far beyond your level of wealth and energy. The right man is a Christian who will make your life easier and whose life you are happy to make easier.

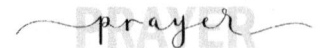

prayer

Here are the seven men whom the Bible indicates were good husbands—the kind you might like to pray for as a lady, and the kind you might like to be as a man.

1. **Joseph** — the Husband of Mary, the mother of Jesus. The New Testament described him as a "just man" (Matthew 1:19), one who obeyed God's commands, did not have sex before marriage, and was protective and supportive towards Mary and Jesus.
2. **Aquila** — he and his wife Priscilla are mentioned together five times in the New Testament—three times his wife's name preceded his, indicating a partnership in ministry and life, and suggesting a

HUSBAND

good marital relationship. Note a woman can lead in the calling to ministry, but in the home her husband is called to lead. When there's a dispute in the home, he should go to God to be guided and solve difficult issues.

3. **Boaz** — From the Book of Ruth, Boaz is seen as a model of kindness, generosity and redemption. He refused to have pre-marital sex with Ruth when given the opportunity, but arranged to be her "kinsman redeemer" to ensure her security and well-being. Boaz was significantly older than Ruth. The Jewish Midrash puts the age gap at a minimum of 40 years.*

4. **Abraham** — While Abraham briefly had a minor wife, Hagar, he is generally seen as faithful to God and to his wife. Both his children Ishmael and Isaac greatly admired him. The entire Middle East admires him today. God said, *"For I know him, that he will command his children and his household after him, and they shall keep the way of the Lord to do JUSTICE..."* (Genesis 18:19 KJ21) A good husband has a strong sense of justice. When he and Sarah disagreed about Ishmael, he sought God who said, *"Listen to her voice."* (Genesis 21:12)

5. **Isaac** — Known for his peaceful nature and his love for Rebekah, he sowed and provided his family in difficult times (See the chapter "Famine"). His glaring weakness was his favoritism towards Esau which caused family strife. What began as a family feud paved the way to many Middle Eastern conflicts between Israel and Esau's descendants the Edomites (modern Jordanians, Arabians, and some rabbis claim the ancient Romans).

6. **Hosea** — His marriage to Gomer, an adulteress who deserted her husband, symbolizes God's love for Israel despite her unfaithfulness. His commitment to his wife despite her infidelity is as a profound example of love and forgiveness.

7. **Josiah** — King Josiah was a good example for every husband and father. God sent Jeremiah the prophet to tell Shallum (aka Jehoahaz) the fourth son of Josiah, *"Think about your father."* But he didn't listen. He was dethroned after only 3 months of rule by Pharaoh

---

* Ruth's age may have been 40 (Ruth Rabbah 4:4; BT Shabbat 113b). Boaz' age may have been 80 (Ruth Rabbah 7:4; Ruth Zuta 4:13).

Necho II and died in prison. My advice is to ponder and pray on what God said about King Josiah:

> **JEREMIAH 22:15-16** (NET) …Just think about your father. He was **content** that he had food and drink. He did what was **just** and right. So things went well with him. **16** He upheld the cause of the **poor and needy**. So things went well for Judah.' The LORD says, 'That is a good example of what it means to **know me**.'

1. Be content. Some people only do things out of discontentment. They don't act till they're uncomfortable, broke, angry or jealous. They're motivated by negative emotions. God wants us to be motivated by positive thoughts and emotions.

2. Be just. Some people assume being content means doing nothing. That is false. Josiah was content, and he did what was just and right. He thought about others and found ways to take care of their needs.

3. This is what it means to know God: To be happy about your life regardless of outward circumstances and to think about the interests of others. This means to be good on the inside and outside. Being a good man requires God inside of you. God will not come inside you until you repent for all your sins and confess your public faith in Jesus as your only Savior.

4. Things went well with him and his followers. Live in this place of balance, and things will go well with you and your family.

PRAY: *Dear Father, I pray for my husband to prosper and be in health, even as his soul prospers (3 John 1:2). Show me how I can acknowledge his good qualities and make his life easier. Open my eyes to be a loving, honoring and supportive wife. I will stay gentle and quiet when I'm tempted to say too much. I trust You to guide him even when I disagree with him. Cause him to discover his destiny.*

May You bless him with the best attributes of Joseph, Aquila, Boaz, Abraham, Isaac, Hosea, and Josiah. These were not perfect men, but godly men who knew how to course-correct when they were wrong. Cause my husband to know You deeply, to be more content with himself and his life, to do what's just and right, so that things will go well with him, in Jesus' Name.

HUSBAND

Every marriage needs to be nurtured. Men naturally focus on work, so after marriage they eventually forget to nurture the relationship, but women also neglect the relationship without acknowledging it. Women focus on the men until babies come along, then they naturally nurture the children and forget their husbands.

Many couples who divorce can't explain what happened to them. They say things like, "We've grown apart" or "We fell out of love." The toxic ones say, "He found somebody else" or "She left me." Actually, long before the divorce, they nurtured something else and forgot to nurture each other. Things die of neglect. They forgot to do the things they used to do when they were dating, then they gave themselves the excuse that they're older now so they don't have to. It's a formula to misery.

Some couples don't divorce, but they no longer stay in the same bed or same room. That's not a marriage. Prayer alone won't fix this. Faith has to be mixed with works.

WAYS I NURTURE MY HUSBAND THAT NO OTHER WOMAN CAN

_____

_____

_____

_____

_____

_____

_____

_____

_____

Most husbands respond to honor. If you're unsure how to nurture him, ask him. He may be surprised. Pray for him to share honestly.

32
JOBS & OPPORTUNITIES

Tip: The worst thing you can do while you don't have a job is do nothing! While you have free time, give God your talents, volunteer for your church, and prove that you can be motivated by a good cause and not only by money.

The second worst thing you can do during a job hunt is to surf the Internet all day. Please stop it if you are spending hours in front of your computer, because 1) the Internet doesn't give people jobs, 2) it will end up *hurting your faith* to wish for jobs you won't get. Limit your time surfing the Net, and only do so AFTER doing adequate spiritual or natural preparation.

Naturally, you need to not be idle. Make sure you have your resume done and proofread by someone mature. Again, find something to do for your church, and He will reward you.

Spiritually, it'd be better for you to spend an hour or two praying in tongues than eight hours a day surfing the Net. If you instead prayed eight hours a day, your faith would be built up, your future would be prayed out, and you would give God the opportunity to speak to you and direct you by His Spirit.

Most people end up finding a good job through personal contact or referral. Getting addresses off the Internet and throwing out 30 applications a week (the shot gun approach) then getting 30 rejection letters is not only demoralizing, it also damages your faith and is a terrible waste of time. Put your efforts elsewhere.

JOBS & OPPORTUNITIES

If you've read the introduction "How to Use This Book" and the first chapter "Basics of Prayer," you will know that you have to build a case for why you should have the job you want. Here are Scriptures to build a case on why you should find a great job or business opportunity.

prayer

2 THESSALONIANS 3:10 For even when we were with you, we commanded you this: If anyone will not work, neither shall he eat.

1 THESSALONIANS 4:11 (NIV) Make it your ambition to lead a quiet life, to mind your own business and to work with your hands, just as we told you,

3 JOHN 1:2 (AKJ) Beloved, I wish above all things that you may prosper and be in health, even as your soul prospers.

MATTHEW 6:32-33 (AKJ) For after all these things [food, clothes, lifestyle, income] the Gentiles seek. For your heavenly Father knows that you need all these things. But seek first the kingdom of God and His righteousness, and all these things shall be added to you.

PROVERBS 10:22 The blessing of the LORD makes one rich, And He adds no sorrow with it.

PROVERBS 13:22 (AKJ) A good man leaves an inheritance to his children's children: and the wealth of the sinner is laid up for the just.

DEUTERONOMY 28:2-3, 5-6, 12-13 (AKJ)

2 And all these blessings shall come on you, and overtake you, if you shall listen to the voice of the LORD your God.

3 Blessed shall you be in the city, and blessed shall you be in the field.

5 Blessed shall be your basket and your store.

6 Blessed shall you be when you come in, and blessed shall you be when you go out.

12 The LORD shall open to you his good treasure, the heaven to give the rain to your land in his season, and to bless all the work of your hand: and you shall lend to many nations, and you shall not borrow.

13 And the LORD shall make you the head, and not the tail; and you shall be above only, and you shall not be beneath; if that you listen to the commandments of the LORD your God, which I command you this day, to observe and to do them:

THE NEXT DREAM JOB OR OPPORTUNITY I WANT:

_____

_____

_____

_____

_____

_____

_____

_____

_____

_____

_____

_____

_____

_____

_____

_____

*For more faith in this area, meditate also on the chapter "Wealth." If you are unfamiliar with the Bible's teaching on financial wisdom, please use the time in between jobs to learn and fortify your understand of this topic. A recommended resource from this ministry is the "**Financial Breakthrough**" series.*

33
JOY

WHAT BRINGS JOY

God wants us to grow in the fruit of joy. Faith brings joy. Justice brings joy. Without doubt believers felt jubilant when they were vindicated. Restoration feels good. The key is to have joy because God is good and just, even when people are wicked and unjust.

ISAIAH 29:19-21 The humble also shall increase their **JOY** in the Lord, and the poor among men shall **REJOICE** in the Holy One of Israel. **20** For **the terrible one is brought to nothing**, The scornful one is consumed, And all who watch for iniquity are **cut off** [Biblical euphemism for die]—**21** Who make a man an offender by a word, And lay a snare for him who reproves in the gate, And turn aside the just by empty words.

(CEB) The poor will again find **JOY** in the Lord, and the neediest of people will **REJOICE** in the holy one of Israel. **20** The **tyrant** will be no more, the **mocker** will perish, and **all who plot** evil will be **eliminated**: **21** all who **incriminate** others wrongly, who **entrap** the judge in the gate, and pointlessly **postpone** justice for the innocent.

ISAIAH 30:29 You shall have a SONG as in the night when a holy festival is kept, and GLADNESS of heart as when one goes with a flute, to come into the mountain of the LORD…

ISAIAH 51:3-4 For the Lord will comfort Zion…JOY and GLADNESS will be found in it, Thanksgiving and the voice of melody. 4…For law will proceed from Me, And I will make My JUSTICE rest As a LIGHT of the peoples.

ISAIAH 56:7 Even them I will bring to My holy mountain, and make them JOYFUL in My house of prayer…For My house shall be called a house of prayer for all nations.

PROVERBS 21:15 (NIV) When Justice is done, it brings JOY to the righteous but terror to evildoers.

PSALM 58:10 (KJV) The righteous shall REJOICE when he teeth vengeance: he shall wash his feet in the blood of the wicked.

ROMANS 14:17 for the kingdom of God is not eating and drinking, but righteousness and peace and JOY in the Holy Spirit.

ROMANS 15:13 Now may the God of hope fill you with all JOY and peace in believing, that you may abound in hope by the power of the Holy Spirit.

1 PETER 1:8 whom having not seen you love. Though now you do not see Him, yet believing, you REJOICE with JOY inexpressible and full of glory,

THINGS THAT INCREASE MY JOY

_____

_____

_____

_____

_____

_____

_____

_____

34
JUSTICE

The Scriptures I will give you are tried and tested. They have brought justice and restoration for people I know. These victories include:

- A Christian school principal who was cheated and harassed by her second-in-charge until she prayed these prayers
- A Christian lawyer whose daughter's friend was murdered and her case went cold until he prayed these prayers.
- A Christian widow who was scammed of her retirement funds and could not get her stolen crypto back, until she prayed these prayers.
- A Christian father who could not see his own children, until he prayed these prayers.

Christians have been told to "turn the other cheek" and never ask God for justice. There is partial truth in that. We are never to take matters into our own hands or seek revenge. We are to forgive and live with a clean heart. But we must quote the whole Scripture.

> **ROMANS 12:19** Beloved, do not avenge yourselves [the Church teaches this currently], but rather give place to wrath [the Church omits teaching this which leads to error]; for it is written, "Vengeance is Mine, I will repay," says the Lord. [The Holy Spirit reveals God's heart for justice and restoration. Do we believe this Scripture in its entirety?]

When Jesus taught His disciples how to pray, He cited an unusual example rarely shown in the Church: a woman who cried day and night, *"Get justice for me from my adversary."* (Luke 18:3). The King James Version says she cried, *"Avenge me."*

How many Christians pray this way? Did Jesus rebuke her? On the contrary, Jesus responded that God the Father would answer this prayer for justice, if certain conditions were met, *"And shall God not avenge His own elect who cry out day and night to Him, though He bears long with them?"* (Luke 18:7)

One of the conditions to sue for justice is that we must be innocent ourselves. We must be just. That means we must believe in divine justice, study how it works and put it to practice.

Judging is difficult work. We start by being just and fair in our own homes. We should carry this spirit into our churches. Currently, few in the Church have heard anything about Biblical justice.

Who Are the Agents of Justice?

There are two places in the Bible that tell us that our future is to become universal judges: **Psalm 149** and **1 Corinthians 6**. Therefore we are judges-in-training. God wants us to learn how to call down justice now.

> **PSALM 149:5-9** Let the saints be joyful in glory; Let them sing aloud on their beds. **6** Let the high praises of God be in their mouth, And a two-edged sword in their hand, **7** To **execute vengeance** on the nations, And punishments on the peoples; **8** To bind their kings with chains, And their nobles with fetters of iron; **9** To **execute on them the written judgment**—This honor have all His saints. Praise the Lord!

We find 3 key principles of justice:

1. A good judge is a **balanced** person: a good judge has to be a worshipper of God *and* a practical person. He is both spiritual

(praises God) and naturally capable (carries a 2-edged sword in his hand).
2. A good judge is **courageous**: he executes, punishes, and binds nobles and kings. He does not play favoritism with the rich and powerful. He does not show contempt for the lowly and poor.
3. A good judge is **just**: a good judge doesn't follow his own bias, prejudice, or a partisan spirit; a good judge follows an objective standard. How can he do that? God gave him the way: he is to faithfully executes the "**written judgment.**"

That means, if you can find it written in the Bible, then you can apply it judicially to a case. Find where it is written!

Liars, Crooks & Criminals

Here is a "written judgment" we've used against liars, cheaters, false accusers, con artists, murderers, character assassins, crooks and criminals. To pray this prayer, you must not be one yourself, or else the judgment you call on others will fall on you! (2 Samuel 16:5, Psalm 17:15-16, Esther 7:10) Make sure you're born again and living clean *before* you pray this!

PSALM 10

6 He has said in his heart, "I shall not be moved; I shall never be in adversity." [The sinner boasts he will not be caught.]

7 His mouth is full of cursing and deceit and oppression; Under his tongue is trouble and iniquity.

8 He sits in the lurking places of the villages; In the secret places he **murders** the innocent; His eyes are secretly fixed on the helpless.

14 But You have seen, for You observe trouble and grief, To **repay** it by Your hand. The helpless commits himself to You; **You are the helper** of the fatherless.

15 Break the arm of the wicked and the evil *man;* Seek out his wickedness until You find none.

16 The Lord *is* King forever and ever [the King was also the Judge in the Bible]; The nations have perished out of His land.

17 Lord, You have heard the desire of the humble; You will prepare their heart; You will cause Your ear to hear,

18 To **do justice** to the fatherless and the oppressed, That the man of the earth may oppress no more. [The "man of earth" refers to a worldly man who lies, hates and murders.]

PSALM 27 (HCSB)

1 The Lord is my light [the symbol of Justice in the Bible] and my salvation —whom should I fear? The Lord is the stronghold of my life—of whom should I be afraid?

2 When evildoers came against me to devour my flesh, my foes and my enemies stumbled and fell.

3 Though an army deploys against me, my heart is not afraid; though a war breaks out against me, still I am confident.

4 I have asked one thing from the Lord; it is what I desire: to dwell in the house of the Lord all the days of my life, gazing on the beauty of the Lord and seeking Him in His temple.

5 For He will **conceal me** in His shelter in the day of adversity; He will **hide me** under the cover of His tent; He will **set me high** on a rock.

6 Then my head will be high above my enemies around me; I will offer sacrifices in His tent with shouts of joy. I will sing and make music to the Lord.

7 Lord, hear my voice when I call; be gracious to me and answer me.

8 My heart says this about You, "You are to seek My face." Lord, I will seek Your face.

13 I am certain that I will **see the Lord's goodness in the land of the living**.

COMMENT: It's important that David had faith to see the Lord's goodness "in the land of the living." That means **in this life**. Don't put God's promises till later. Believe for His blessings in the "here and now."

JUSTICE

PSALM 94 (KJV)

12 Blessed is the man whom You instruct, O Lord, And teach out of Your law,

13 That You may give him **rest from the days of adversity**, Until the pit is dug for the wicked.

14 For the Lord will not cast off His people…

15 But judgment [JUSTICE] will return to righteousness, And all the upright in heart will follow it.

16 Who will rise up for me against the evildoers? Who will stand up for me against the workers of iniquity?

17 Unless **the Lord had been my help**, my soul had almost dwelt in silence.

22 But **the Lord has been my defense**, And my God the rock of my refuge.

23 He has brought on them their own iniquity, And shall **cut them off** in their own wickedness; The Lord our God shall cut them off.

It's important that David said his faith was to see the Lord's goodness "in the land of the living." That means *in this life*. Often God's people put God's blessings off to Heaven. But the Lord invites us to believe for victory the "here and now."

PSALM 144 (KJV)

11 **Rid me**, and **deliver me** from the hand of strange children, whose mouth speaketh vanity, and their right hand is a right hand of falsehood…14 That our oxen may be strong to labour; that there be no breaking in, nor going out; that there be **no complaining** in our streets.

PSALM 118 (HCSB)

5 I called to the Lord in distress; **the Lord answered me** and put me in a spacious place.6 The Lord is for me; **I will not be afraid**. What can man do to me? 7 The Lord is my helper, Therefore, I will **look in triumph** on those who hate me.

COMMENT: Once you've prayed, you need to praise God vengeance is now in His hands. It's done. Don't bother to pray again in fear. When you least feel like it, when the problems keep nagging you, you need to "look in triumph" towards your prayer answer. Be assured that the Lord is for you. He is Your advocate. He defends you. As soon as you release faith through your words, God begins to work to prove these Psalms true.

PSALM 143:9-12

9 Deliver me from my enemies, O Lord! I have fled to you for refuge. **10 Teach me to do your will**, for you are my God! Let your good Spirit lead me on level ground! **11** For your name's sake, O Lord, preserve my life! In your righteousness bring my soul out of trouble! **12** And in your steadfast love you will **cut off** my enemies, and you will **destroy** all the adversaries of my soul, for I am your servant.

JUSTICE ISSUES THAT ARE IMPORTANT TO ME

_____

_____

_____

_____

_____

_____

BALANCE: *In life, you have to pick your battles. Not every cause is yours. Some ministers got out of their lanes by getting involved in other people's ministries or business. They felt a sense of self-righteousness about it. They felt justified to criticize others who appeared wrong. Unless it affects you, stay out of these squabbles. It's NOT your race. Run your race! (Hebrews 12:1)*

Search for more Scriptures on "Justice" in these chapters: Avenge Me, Court, Deliverance, Enemies, and Lawsuits & Legal Battles.

35
KINDNESS

One of the greatest blessings in life is to have someone with authority show kindness to you. To receive this, I make it a practice to sow kindness.

Being kind is not natural to everyone. Many powerful people are no longer kind. Power tends to make people unkind. *Many politicians could pray more for kindness.* Many aged ministers are no loner kind. The experience of ministry can make seasoned ministers lose patience, gentleness and kindness. Then anointed minsters get sick and troubled without realizing why. May I never become that way!

I activate kindness by meditating on instances of kindness in the Bible, then speaking forth those Scriptures over and over until the reality sinks in.

GENESIS 24:12 Then he said, "O Lord God of my master Abraham, please give me success this day, and show KINDNESS to my master Abraham."

Kindness = Success.

This is the first instance of the word "kindness" in the Bible—Abraham's servant Eleazer asking for God's kindness. In this instance, God's kindness meant finding a good wife for Abraham's son Isaac. His kindness was equated with success.

For many of us, simply being kinder would equate to greater success in our personal lives. Kindness is a big deal to God. So I make it a habit to pray for kindness.

JOSHUA 2:12-13 [Rahab the prostitute in Jericho asked the two Jewish spies for kindness] Now therefore, I beg you, swear to me by the Lord, since I have shown you KINDNESS, that you also will show KINDNESS to my father's house, and give me a true token, **13** and spare my father, my mother, my brothers, my sisters, and all that they have, and deliver our lives from death.

Kindness = To be spared from suffering and punishment.

What if Rahab had been unkind to the strangers? She and everyone she loved would have perished.

RUTH 2:20 [Naomi acknowledged God showed kindness to Ruth] Then Naomi said to her daughter-in-law, "Blessed be he of the Lord, who has not forsaken His KINDNESS to the living and the dead!" And Naomi said to her, "This man is a relation of ours, one of our close relatives."

Kindness = To meet a rescuer, to have a divine appointment.

2 SAMUEL 2:5-6 [David recognized and rewarded kindness] So David sent messengers to the men of Jabesh Gilead, and said to them, "You are blessed of the Lord, for you have shown this KINDNESS to your lord, to Saul, and have buried him. **6** And now may the Lord show KINDNESS and truth to you. I also will repay you this KINDNESS, because you have done this thing.

Kindness = Giving a proper burial for and honoring the dead, even if he was not a good person. Kindness gets rewarded!

PSALM 117:2 For His MERCIFUL KINDNESS is great toward us, And the truth of the Lord endures forever.

ISAIAH 54:8-10 With a little wrath I hid My face from you for a moment; But with EVERLASTING KINDNESS I will have mercy on you," Says the Lord, your Redeemer. **9** For this is like the waters of Noah to Me; For as I have sworn that I the waters of Noah would no longer cover the earth, so have I sworn that I would not be angry with you, nor rebuke you. **10** For the mountains shall depart and the hills be removed, but My KINDNESS shall not depart from you, nor shall

KINDNESS

My covenant of peace be removed," says the Lord, who has mercy on you.

Kindness = No repeated pain, the promise (covenant) of peace, a guarantee of safety. Here's the same promise in the New Testament.

MATTHEW 12:20 (NIV) A bruised reed he will not break, and a smoldering wick he will not snuff out, till he has brought justice through to victory.

MATTHEW 12:20 (Aramaic) He will not break off a fractured reed, and the lamp that flickers he will not extinguish until he will bring the verdict of innocence,

JOEL 2:13 ....For He is gracious and merciful, Slow to anger, and of great KINDNESS; And He relents from doing harm.

Kindness = the opposite of anger. A kind person is very slow to anger and reluctant to threaten.

JONAH 4:2 (KJV) ...for I knew that thou art a gracious God, and merciful, slow to anger, and of great KINDNESS, and repentest thee of the evil.

ROMANS 2:4 (NAS) ...the KINDNESS of God leads you to repentance (The King James Version says the "goodness of God" leads you to repentance.)

PSALM 40:11 (KJV) Withhold not thou thy tender mercies from me, O Lord: let thy lovingkindness and thy truth continually preserve me.

Kindness without truth would be abuse. Being nice without confronting character flaws and addressing reality is negligence. Kindness needs to be counterbalanced with truth. Together they preserve a person's soul.

Put another way, people perish, become depressed and age prematurely when they forsake two things: kindness and truth. Having only one is not enough protection.

PSALM 69:16 (KJV) Hear me, O Lord; for thy lovingkindness is good: turn unto me according to the multitude of thy tender mercies.

Kindness is good.

GALATIANS 5:22-23 But the fruit of the Spirit is love, joy, peace, long-suffering, kindness, goodness, faithfulness, gentleness, self-control. Against such there is no law.

Kindness = the 5th fruit of the born again spirit. That means it can grow if you water it and nurture it. The King James Version translates kindness as "gentleness." To be kind is to be gentle.

EPHESIANS 4:32 And be ye KIND one to another, tenderhearted, forgiving one another, even as God for Christ's sake hath forgiven you.

Kindness = Forgiveness. Kind Christians are forgiving.

Do you think God would ask us to do something He isn't unwilling to do? No, that would be unfair, and God is never unfair. Since God asks us to be kind and forgiving, then we can be assured that He is kind and forgiving to us!

Kindness has great rewards. Pray for the fruit of kindness to grow in you!

WAYS I WILL BE KIND

_____
_____
_____
_____
_____
_____
_____
_____
_____
_____
_____

36
LAWSUITS & LEGAL BATTLES

*A*re you going to court? First read the chapter on "Court," then come back to this chapter to pray!

Tip: I've seen God help people who faced impossible legal battles and even multi-million dollar lawsuits. They came through with victory! If you want victory, you have to get serious with God and learn how to apply God's Word correctly.

When you face a legal battle or lawsuit, don't be afraid. It's an opportunity to trust God and watch God show Himself strong on your behalf. God knows the judicial system better than anybody else - He is both Judge and Advocate!

If you are actually guilty of wrongdoing, waste no time to repent before God, then accept the gift of acquittal through Jesus Christ's sacrifice. He was punished for you. Then go to human court humbly, knowing that you have been forgiven by God and His mercy was undeserved.

If on the other hand, you have been wrongly accused, you must also get on your knees and release that accusing party. Jesus said, "Pray for your enemies." Yes, the world is full of injustice. It's not God's fault. It's the result of living among sinners. Jesus lived a perfect life and yet He was falsely accused, wrongly tried, and unjustly sentenced to death. Jesus understands your situation. Yet He forgave those who beat Him and crucified Him. You can win a case even before the court case starts, if you win it first with God. Walk in love towards your enemies because Jesus did.

If you are accusing someone of wrongdoing, you have to forgive that person first. Christians sometimes wonder if they are allowed to go to court to rectify a matter that could not be solved outside of court. Understand this: going to court is not wrong, but hating someone is! Seeking justice on earth is not wrong, but seeking revenge is! You have to go to court with love. If you can stand before God with a clean and peaceful heart, God will be on your side. Just remember, on this earth there is not always perfect justice, but in Heaven there will be.

One more important note, Christians should not take Christians to court. Paul wrote, "When one of you has a complaint against another, does he dare to take the matter before those who are unrighteous and not before the saints? ...one brother goes to court against another brother, and before unbelieving judges, at that! The very fact that you have lawsuits among yourselves is already a defeat for you. Why not rather just accept the wrong? Why not rather be cheated?" (1 Cor 6:1-8 ISV)

Christians should settle matters Scripturally: approach the offending party privately first, then with two or three Christian witnesses if private communication fails, then in front of the whole church as a last resort. Few Christian practice Matthew 18 properly. That's why they're in unnecessary strife. Instead of confronting, they ignore a small problem until it becomes a big one. Instead of talking about the problem, go talk to the person directly and discreetly. You will find God's grace is there when you do it God's way.

When the Bible says Christians should not take Christians to court, that doesn't refer to everybody who calls themselves Christian. I don't believe a liar or a thief can be a Christian, because the Bible says, "All liars shall have their part in the lake which burneth with fire" (Revelation 21:8) and thieves will not "inherit the kingdom of God" (1 Corinthians 6:10).

If a so-called Christian swindles you of money, forgive the person, don't hate them, then take them to court. You are not hating someone by taking them to court; you are letting the wheel of justice turn. You may be saving other people's lives or at least spare them from being swindled again by a sinner who should be held accountable and brought to justice. A good court is God's minister for justice on the earth.

Nevertheless genuine Christians can sometimes have misunderstandings with each other. These should NOT be brought to court. Learn to fight *for* one another, instead of fight *against* one another. Resolve issues directly, immediately, and amicably, as Christians who will spend eternity together. God's love never fails!

If you fail to resolve a case immediately, there is a statute of limitation to protect the accused (the defendant) in many legal jurisdictions. It ranges from 1 to 10 years depending on the type of crime and the state. There are exceptions for capital crimes, terrorism, and sexual offenses against children.

It's unjust to bring up a crime against someone after 40 years. The Biblical standard is Moses. He murdered an Egyptian, was charged with the crime in the jurisdiction of Egypt, then fled to Midian for 40 years. When he returned to Egypt, no one in Egypt brought a criminal charge against him for something that happened 40 years earlier.

How long was the statute of limitation in Egypt? It could have been far less than 40 years. Or it may more likely have been based on the life of the Pharaoh. The Bible prohibits the "revenger of blood" from pursuing a man accused of involuntary manslaughter if he's hiding in a "city of refuge" or after the death of the high priest (Numbers 35:25-28, Joshua 20:6). When the high priest dies, the accused is free to go home, and be protected from any further charges or punishment.

prayer

Prayer for Victory and Vindication

PROVERBS 21:1 (AKJ) The king's heart is in the hand of the LORD, as the rivers of water: he turns it wherever he will.

PRAY: *If the heart of the king is in the hand of the Lord, how much more is the heart of the judge, the prosecutor, the lawyers, the witnesses, everyone who is involved in this legal case. Like a river of water, turn their hearts in my favor, in Jesus' Name!*

ISAIAH 54:17 (AKJ) No weapon that is formed against you shall prosper; and every tongue that shall rise against you in judgment you shall condemn. This is the heritage of the servants of the LORD, and their righteousness is of me, said the LORD.

PRAY: *No weapon or false accusation formed against me shall prosper. Every lying tongue is condemned! My protection is a heritage of the servants of the Lord. No lie can live forever. Truth will prevail, in Jesus' Name!*

1 JOHN 2:1 (AKJ) My little children, these things write I to you, that you sin not. And if any man sin, we have an advocate with the Father, Jesus Christ the righteous:

CONFESS: *Jesus is my Advocate, He is my lawyer. He is on my side, pleading my case, defending me against the accusations of the devil. They will not stick because Jesus is my Defense!*

1 JOHN 4:4 (AKJ) You are of God, little children, and have overcome them: because greater is he that is in you, than he that is in the world.

CONFESS: *Greater is God who is in me than all the evil that is in the world. Greater is the Advocate in me than the accuser that is in the world. Greater is the Peace that is in me than the turmoil that is in the world. I have overcome because the Overcomer lives in me!*

MATTHEW 5:25 (God's Word) Make peace quickly with your opponent while you are on the way to court with him. Otherwise, he will hand you over to the judge. Then the judge will hand you over to an officer, who will throw you into prison.

ROMANS 12:18 (AKJ) If it be possible, as much as lies in you, live peaceably with all men. (ESV) If possible, so far as it depends on you, live peaceably with all. (World English) If it is possible, as much as it is up to you, be at peace with all men.

PSALM 37:6 He shall bring forth your righteousness as the **light**, And your justice as the **noonday**.

(NLT) He will make your innocence radiate like the **dawn**, and the justice of your cause will shine like the noonday **sun**.

(NIV) He will make your righteous reward shine like the **dawn**, your vindication like the noonday **sun**.

THE ORDERS/ OUTCOMES I BELIEVE ARE JUST

_____

_____

_____

_____

Praying for the Custody of Children

PSALM 127:3 Behold, children are a heritage from the Lord, The fruit of the womb is a reward.

ISAIAH 8:18 (KJV) Behold, I and the children whom the LORD hath given me are for signs and for wonders in Israel from the LORD of hosts, which dwelleth in mount Zion.

PSALM 37:25 "I have not seen the righteous forsaken, nor his seed begging bread." [Nor begging for time, holidays, travel, etc. with one parent or with children.]

JOSHUA 24:15 (KJV) ...but as for me and my house, we will serve the LORD.

Praying for BREAKTHROUGH in Difficult Situations

ISAIAH 58:8-9 (NIV) Then your light will **break forth** like the dawn, and your healing will quickly appear; then your righteousness will go before you, and the glory of the Lord will be your rear guard. 9 Then you will call, and the Lord will answer; you will cry for help, and he will say: Here am I.

2 SAMUEL 5:20 (NAS) So David came to Baal-perazim and defeated them [Philistines] there; and he said, "The LORD has **broken through** my enemies before me like the **breakthrough** of waters." Therefore he named that place Baal-perazim.

ACTION: *Remember to give God glory for the victory! How? Glorify Him both privately and publicly. Glorify Jesus for saving you by attending church, paying your tithes (which will typically be far less than your legal fees—thank God for it!), and testifying to non-Christians how the Lord was good to you.*

37

LEADER'S PRAYER

Leaders Pray for Others

PHILIPPIANS 2:13-16 [Pray this for someone you're leading.]

13 for it is God who works in you both to will and to do for His good pleasure. **14** Do all things without complaining and disputing,

15 that you may become blameless and harmless, children of God without fault in the midst of a crooked and perverse generation, among whom you shine as lights in the world,

16 holding fast the word of life, so that I may rejoice in the day of Christ that I have not run in vain or labored in vain.

PRAY: *Lord, work in _____ both to will and to do Your good pleasure. May they do all things without complaining and disputing. May they become blameless and harmless, and shine as the light of Christ in the world. As they hold fast the Word of Life, I rejoice that I have made a good disciple. I have not run in vain or labored in vain. As I make more disciples, let me experience the joy of my labors. (John 4:36)*

PSALM 144:11-15 (KJV)

11 Rid me, and deliver me from the hand of strange children, whose mouth speaketh vanity, and their right hand is a right hand of falsehood: [I pray enemies away from the flock!]

LEADER'S PRAYER

12 That our **sons** may be as plants grown up in their youth; that our **daughters** may be as corner stones, polished after the similitude of a palace: [I pray for my spiritual children, my disciples, to grow up in Christ.]

13 That our garners may be full, affording all manner of store [I pray we prosper]: that our **sheep** may bring forth thousands and ten thousands in our streets: [I pray that sheep beget sheep! Disciples make disciples!]

14 That our **oxen** [leaders, staff, helpers] may be strong to labour; that there be no breaking in, nor going out; that there be no complaining in our streets. [I pray that our church leaders be strong and work hard without complaining. I pray grumblers go away in Jesus' Name!]

15 Happy is that people, that is in such a case: yea, happy is that people, whose God is the LORD. [I pray for our leaders, volunteers, partners, and church members to be happy in ministry and joyful in obeying the Lord.]

EZEKIEL 36:10-11, 37-38

10 I will **multiply** men upon you, all the house of Israel, all of it; and the cities shall be inhabited and the ruins rebuilt.

11 I will **multiply** upon you man and beast; and they shall **increase** and bear young; I will make you inhabited as in former times, and do better for you than at your beginnings. Then you shall know that I am the Lord.

37 'Thus says the Lord God: "I will also let the house of Israel inquire of Me to do this for them: I will **increase** their men like a flock.

38 Like a flock offered as holy sacrifices, like the flock at Jerusalem on its feast days, so shall the ruined cities **be filled** with flocks of men. Then they shall know that I am the Lord."'"

PRAY: *Father, You promised church growth! Multiply our men [church members] and our beasts [the servants in the church]. Increase our church [ministry] with men like a flock, as a holy flock. Let dormant and dead ministries be revived and filled with flocks of men. Then everyone will know that You are our Lord.*

MATTHEW 16:18 And I also say to you that you are Peter, and on this rock I will build My church, and the gates of Hades shall not prevail against it.

PRAY: *Lord, You said You are building Your church and the gates of Hell shall not prevail against it. Thank You for building the members of this church.*

LUKE 10:2 Then He said to them, "The harvest truly is great, but the laborers are few; therefore pray the Lord of the harvest to send out laborers into His harvest.

PRAY: *You said the harvest is plenteous, but the laborers are few. I pray the Lord of the harvest that You would send out more laborers into Your harvest. Send forth more five-fold ministers, anointed worship leaders, choir masters, web developers, IT experts, social media marketers, children's church workers, youth leaders, street ministry teams, event organizers, fundraisers, and missionaries, [name your ministry needs].*

PSALM 110:3 (NAS) Thy people will volunteer freely in the day of Thy power; in holy array, from the womb of the dawn, Thy youth are to Thee as the dew.

PRAY: *This is the day of Your power, therefore Your people shall be volunteers. They will serve gladly and minister freely. Our youth will live holy, purposeful, and motivated lives, in Jesus' Name.*

EPHESIANS 4:15-16 (NAS) but speaking the truth in love, we are to grow up in all aspects into Him, who is the head, even Christ, **16** from whom the whole body, being fitted and held together by that which every joint supplies, according to the proper working of each individual part, causes the growth of the body for the building up of itself in love.

PRAY: *I speak the truth in love. Our staff and volunteers speak the truth in love, therefore we grow up in all aspects into Him, who is the head, even Christ. We are fitted and held together by strong bonds and flexible joints, and each individual part working together causes the growth of the Body of Christ. Our leaders are building our church up in love.*

ACTS 6:7 Then the word of God spread, and the number of the disciples multiplied greatly in Jerusalem, and a great many of the priests were obedient to the faith.

PRAY: *May the Word of God spread through my life and ministry. May the number of disciples multiply greatly in my church, and may the ministers we raise up be obedient to the faith.*

To learn how Paul prayed for others, read the Ephesian prayers which are explained in the chapter "Difficult People."

38
LORD'S PRAYER

The Lord's Prayer

Our Father who art in heaven,

hallowed be Thy name.

Thy kingdom come,

Thy will be done

on earth, as it is in heaven.

Give us this day our daily bread,

and forgive us our trespasses,

as we forgive those who trespass against us,

and lead us not into temptation,

but deliver us from evil [*and evil people*].

For Thine is the kingdom, and the power, and the glory,

forever and ever. Amen.

39
LOVE

Tip: *If there's one sure way to make love grow, it's to confess love. Whether you want love to grow in your marriage or your life as a believer, these are the best Scriptures to speak. Where possible, say the word "I" instead of the word "love". For instance, instead of "love endures long and is patient and kind.. love is not rude," say, "I endure long and am patient and kind… I am not rude…"*

ROMANS 5:5 (KJV) The love of God is shed abroad in our hearts by the Holy Ghost which is given unto us.

SAY: *The God-kind-of love is in me! I do not have to pray for it; it's already in me. I let God's love guide my decisions.*

> **1 CORINTHIANS 13:4-8** Love suffers long and is kind; love does not envy; love does not parade itself, is not puffed up; **5** does not behave rudely, does not seek its own, is not provoked, thinks no evil; **6** does not rejoice in iniquity, but rejoices in the truth; **7** bears all things, believes all things, hopes all things, endures all things. **8** Love never fails.

1 CORINTHIANS 13:4-8 (Amplified)

4 Love endures long and is patient and kind; love never is envious nor boils over with jealousy; is not boastful or vainglorious, does not display itself haughtily.

5 It is not conceited—arrogant and inflated with pride; it is not rude (unmannerly), and does not act unbecomingly. Love [God's love in us] does not insist on its own rights or its own way, for it is not self-seeking; it is not touchy or fretful or resentful; it takes no account of the evil done to it—pays no attention to a suffered wrong.

6 It does not rejoice at injustice and unrighteousness, but rejoices when right and truth prevail.

7 Love bears up under anything and everything that comes, is ever ready to believe the best of every person, its hopes are fadeless under all circumstances and it endures everything [without weakening].

8 Love never fails—never fades out or becomes obsolete or comes to an end.

1 CORINTHIANS 13:4-8 (NIV) Love is patient, love is kind. It does not envy, it does not boast, it is not proud. **5** It is not rude, it is not self-seeking, it is not easily angered, it keeps no record of wrongs. **6** Love does not delight in evil but rejoices with the truth. **7** It always protect, always trusts, always hopes, always perseveres. **8** Love never fails.

1 CORINTHIANS 13:4-8 (J.B. Phillips)

This love of which I speak is slow to lose patience—it looks for a way of being constructive. It is not possessive: it is neither anxious to impress nor does it cherish inflated ideas of its own importance. Love has good manners and does not pursue selfish advantage. It is not touchy. It does not compile statistics of evil or gloat over the wickedness of other people. On the contrary, it is glad with all good men when Truth prevails. Love knows no limit to its endurance, no end to its trust, no fading of its hopes: it can outlast anything. It is, in fact, the one thing that still stands when all else has fallen.

1 CORINTHIANS 14:1 Pursue love, and desire spiritual gifts, but especially that you may prophesy.

SAY: *I put love before spiritual gifts. The anointing is on love. The Anointing flows where love goes. I will let love lead. The greatest expression of love is giving. I'm quick to forgive and quick to give. I am ever ready to believe the best of every person. I'll just walk in love, praise God, keep the victory, and keep on shouting! Love can never fail!*

HOW I WILL LOVE OTHERS MORE

40

MIRACLES

Do you need a miracle? The Christian life starts with believing a miracle: the resurrection of Jesus Christ. It continues through a series of miracles. Miracles have been such a part of my Christian life that I sometimes feel like Peter walking on water. I know it's not me doing it. God enables me. Our calling is to believe for the impossible!

MATTHEW 14:28-29 [Peter said] "Lord, if it is You, command me to come to You on the water." **29** So He said, "Come." And when Peter had come down out of the boat, he walked on the water to go to Jesus.

PRAY: *Lord Jesus, you bid Peter to come walk on water. Call me to walk above my circumstances. Help me to rise above what's normal and possible, and experience the supernatural and the impossible (in man's eyes). One word from You is enough.*

MARK 9:22-23 [the father of a sick, mute, epileptic boy said to Jesus]...But if You can do anything, have compassion on us and help us." **23** Jesus said to him, "If you can believe, ALL things are POSSIBLE to him who believes."

LUKE 1:37 For with God NOTHING shall be IMPOSSIBLE.

COMMENT: Why do some people see more miracles than others? The first condition to experiencing miracles is to make sure you are with God. Make sure you are on God's side. Don't fight Him. Walk with Him. Are you born again by the Blood of Jesus? Are you obeying Jesus?

PRAY: *Lord, when my will collides with Your will, let Your will prevail. I give You permission to intervene in my life. I ask You to do miracles in me and through me. I thank Jesus who made it possible for me to be washed clean by His Blood, so I can walk away from the filth of sin and walk a supernatural Christian life—I can walk on water like Peter did.*

MATTHEW 17:20 [Jesus explained why His disciples could not get a miracle]....So Jesus said to them, "Because of your unbelief; for assuredly, I say to you, if you have faith as a mustard seed, you will say to this mountain, 'Move from here to there,' and it will move; and nothing will be impossible for you.

Unbelief, skepticism, cynicism and sarcasm hinder miracles. King David experienced many miracles against overwhelming odds when he was a nobody (before he was king). You can hear his heart and how he prayed by studying the Book of Psalms.

PSALM 31

1 In You, O Lord, I put my trust; Let me never be ashamed; Deliver me in Your righteousness.

2 Bow down Your ear to me, Deliver me speedily...

4 Pull me out of the net which they have secretly laid for me, For You are my strength.

5 Into Your hand I commit my spirit...

15 My times are in Your hand; Deliver me from the hand of my enemies, And from those who persecute me.

16 Make Your face shine upon Your servant; Save me for Your mercies' sake.

17 Do not let me be ashamed, O Lord, for I have called upon You; Let the wicked be ashamed; Let them be silent in the grave.

18 Let the lying lips be put to silence, Which speak insolent things proudly and contemptuously against the righteous.

19 Oh, **how great is Your goodness**, Which You have laid up for those who fear You...

20 You shall hide them in the secret place of Your presence From the plots of man; You shall keep them secretly in a pavilion From the strife of tongues.

PRAY: *My times are in Your hand. Allow me to see how great is Your goodness, which You have laid up for those who fear You. Hide me the secret place of Your presence from the plots of my enemies. Keep me secretly in Your pavilion from the strife of tongues. It is a miracle to be shielded from human complaints and accusations. Into Your hand I commit my spirit—save me in Jesus' Name.*

INEXPLICABLE MIRACLES IN MY LIFE

_____
_____
_____
_____
_____
_____
_____
_____
_____
_____
_____
_____
_____
_____
_____
_____
_____

41
MORNING PRAISE

Tip: It is good to wake up in the morning with praise on our lips. We can make a decision to be joyful from the first second we get up. Here are 3-habit-forming Scriptures:

PSALM 5:3 My voice shalt thou hear in the morning, O LORD; in the morning will I direct my prayer unto thee, and will look up.

PSALM 55:17 Evening, and morning, and at noon, will I pray, and cry aloud: and he shall hear my voice.

MARK 1:35 (NIV) Very early in the morning, while it was still dark, Jesus got up, left the house and went off to a solitary place, where he prayed.

MY MORNING PRAISE

PSALM 118:24 This is the day the Lord has made; We will rejoice and be glad in it.

Each morning I try to let my knees be the first part of me to touch the floor. I kneel and say:

> *"Good morning, Holy Spirit! This is the day the Lord has made; I will rejoice and be glad in it!"*

MORNING PRAISE

Then I confess the Scriptures below, which I believe have been answered multiple times over.

ISAIAH 50:4-5 (KJV) The Lord God hath given me the tongue of the learned, that I should know how to speak a word in season to him that is weary: he wakeneth [me] morning by morning, he wakeneth mine ear to hear as the learned. **5** The Lord God hath opened mine ear, and I was not rebellious, neither turned away back.

ISAIAH 51:7, 12, 16 (KJV)

7 Hearken unto me, ye that know righteousness, the people in whose heart is my law; fear ye not the reproach of men, neither be ye afraid of their revilings.

12 I, even I, am he that comforteth you: who art thou, that thou shouldest be afraid of a man that shall die, and of the son of man which shall be made as grass;

16 And I have put my words in thy mouth, and I have covered thee in the shadow of mine hand, that I may plant the heavens, and lay the foundations of the earth, and say unto Zion (Israel/ USA/ Australia/ Thailand/ _____ [insert your country]), Thou art my people.

LAMENTATIONS 3:22-28, 32 (KJV)

22 It is of the Lord's mercies that we are not consumed, because his compassions fail not.

23 They are new EVERY morning: GREAT is thy faithfulness.

24 The Lord is my portion, saith my soul; therefore will I hope in him.

25 The Lord is good unto them that wait for him [to me who waits for Him], to the soul that seeketh him.

27 It is good for a man that he bear the yoke in his youth.

28 He sitteth alone and keepeth silence, because he hath borne it upon him.

PSALM 16:11 (KJV)

11 Thou wilt shew me the path of life: in thy presence is fulness of joy; at thy right hand there are pleasures for evermore.

PSALM 17:15 (KJV) As for me, I will behold thy face in righteousness: I shall be satisfied, when I AWAKE, with thy likeness.

(NIV) As for me, I will be vindicated and will see your face; when I AWAKE, I will be satisfied with seeing your likeness.

(NET) As for me, because I am innocent I will see your face; when I AWAKE you will reveal yourself to me.

ACTS 2:25-26,28 (KJV, Peter quotes David's words as recorded in Psalm 16:9-11)

25 I foresaw the Lord always before my face, for he is on my right hand, that I should not be moved:

26 Therefore did my heart rejoice, and my tongue was glad; moreover also my flesh shall rest in hope:

28 Thou hast made known to me the ways of life; thou shalt make me full of joy with thy countenance.

BEFORE WALKING OUT THE DOOR

This is what I say almost every time I leave my home:

> *"Thank You, Father, for making me a light to the Gentiles, brining salvation to the ends of the earth. Thank You for going ahead of me to make the crooked places straight. The steps of a good man are ordered by the Lord—thank You for ordering my steps and my stops. I believe all things are working together for my good who love You and am called according to Your purpose. No weapon formed against me shall prosper and every tongue that rises up against me in judgment, I shall condemn. Give me spiritual children all over the world, in Jesus' Name." (Isaiah 49:6, 45:2, Acts 13:47, Psalm 37:23, Luke 3:5, Romans 8:28, Mark 10:30)*

For "Goodnight" Scriptures, see the chapter "Sleep."

42
NATION

> **1 TIMOTHY 2:1-2** (TLB) Here are my directions: Pray much for others; plead for God's mercy upon them; give thanks for all he is going to do for them. **2** Pray in this way for kings and all others who are in authority over us, or are in places of high responsibility, so that we can live in peace and quietness, spending our time in godly living and thinking much about the Lord.

Tip: If we would obey these directions from the Holy Spirit, we would see success in prayer! Our prayer failures often come from the fact that we pray first for ourselves and our needs. But God said FIRST of ALL, pray for others who are in authority and in places of high responsibility, which include our missionaries, pastors, secular leaders, elected officials, intelligence agencies, judges and police. Then we may pray for our church, family and our own needs.

PRAY: Heavenly Father, I come before You in the Name of Jesus on behalf of the United States of America / _____ (name your nation). I pray for a shield of divine protection over this country; for insight into and the uncovering of all criminal and terrorist activities, including at governmental and judicial levels. I rebuke any spirit of fear and terror. It has no place here.

Father, You said the heart of the king is in the hand of the Lord; like a river of water, You turn it wherever You will (Proverbs 21:1 ESV). So I ask You to turn the hearts and minds of the

US President _____

Israeli Prime Minister _____

Australian Prime Minister _____

British Prime Minister _____

Jordanian King _____

Salvadoran President _____

Saudi King/ Prince _____

Thai King/ Prime Minister _____

and (VP, General, Judge, etc.) _____

I pray for the wisdom of God to guide them to make the right decisions. I also pray for their divine health and strength.

I thank You, Lord, for bringing change to the politics of our nation. Thank You for changing the voices of influence to speak in agreement with Your Word. I ask You to send laborers, filled with the Spirit of wisdom and justice, to surround our leaders with godly counsel and advice. I also ask You to remove from positions of authority those who stubbornly oppose righteousness and justice, and replace them with men and women who will follow You and Your appointed course for this nation.

Your Word declares, "Blessed is the nation whose God is the Lord" (Psalm 33:12). I receive Your blessing and declare with my mouth that Your people dwell safely in this land and they prosper abundantly. I give thanks that our government is upon Jesus' shoulder, and knowledge is pleasant to our politicians. Discretion watches over them. Understanding keeps them and delivers them from the way of evil men. Lord, give them a heart to do Your perfect will, and direct their decisions for the benefit of the Gospel, the Church and families. Expose corruption, evil plots, secret agendas, and purge our land of godless men like Esther did Haman.

You said in Your Word that if Your people would humble themselves, and pray, seek Your face and turn from their wicked ways, You would heal the

NATION

land (2 Chronicles 7:14). So Lord, I repent for the sins of this nation. I pray that You would cleanse us and forgive us for idolatry, witchcraft and every kind of disobedience. Grant this nation a spirit of repentance and obedience. Cover us with Your mercy. As we turn back to You, O Lord, I believe the land is being healed.

As we enter the final hours of the last day, I ask for miracles, signs, wonders, gifts, demonstrations and distributions of the Holy Spirit to be strong in operation. Let believers in _____ (my nation) and in every neighboring land be unified to stand in love and faith in the Lord Jesus Christ, so that Your glory may be revealed in all the Earth.

I thank You that the Good News of Jesus Christ is being published in our land, and Your Word prevails and grows mightily in the hearts and lives of the people. Christian TV, radio, publications, apps, websites, podcasts, and public meetings grow unhindered, unobstructed and uncensored. I pray that all citizens have a chance to be saved and that the saved will grow up spiritually—we are coming to the knowledge of the truth. I declare that Jesus is Lord over _____ (my nation).

I declare that Australia is the Great South Land of the Holy Spirit, as prophesied by Portuguese explorer Pedro Fernandez de Quiros and British Apostle Smith Wigglesworth. Australia will experience the last revival before Jesus returns.

Thank You, Lord, that these requests of ours come to pass. I believe You are giving us the miracle of national salvation, in Jesus' Name. Amen!

> **1 TIMOTHY 2:1-4** (KJV) I exhort therefore, that, FIRST of ALL, supplications, prayers, intercessions, and giving of thanks, be made for all men; **2** For kings, and for all that are in authority; that we may lead a quiet and peaceable life in all godliness and honesty. **3** For this is good and acceptable in the sight of God our Saviour; **4** Who will have all men to be saved, and to come unto the knowledge of the truth.

Related prayers are in chapters "Revival" and "World."

43
NEW YEAR

Each year I host a New Year's Eve Party. I write a prophetic declaration each year and print it for all the guests. At around midnight, my guests and I declare the Holy Scriptures to welcome the New Year. It has been a good practice.

One way you can write your own prayer is using the Psalm-Year Code. The theory is that each Psalm corresponds to a year starting from the 20th century. Psalm is the 19th book of the Bible, so it represents "19_ _". Each chapter represents a corresponding prophetic year. So Psalm 1 = 1901. Psalm 48 = 1948. Psalm 100 = 2000. Psalm 125 = 2025. And so on.

Examples of futuristic Psalms (as of the publishing of this book) will be given at the end.

> **LUKE 21:36** Watch therefore, and pray always that you may be counted worthy to escape all these things that will come to pass, and to stand before the Son of Man.

PRAY: *I watch and pray this year more than ever before. Heavenly Father, count me worthy to escape the Tribulation and to stand before Your Son - my Lord, my God - Jesus Christ.*

NEW YEAR

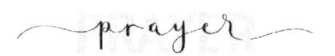

prayer

NEW YEAR PRAYER 1: FAMILY PRAYER

Dear Heavenly Father, we approach You in the Name of our Lord Jesus Christ. Your Word declares, *Thou crownest the year with thy goodness...* (Psalm 65:11). Therefore we join together as a family to say that this New Year is Your Year. This New Year was foreordained by God, is sanctified by Jesus' blood, and shall be blessed by the Holy Spirit. It is not a time for panic, but a time for rejoicing! It is not a time for worrying, but a time for serving the Lord! You will be more glorified in this New Year than in any other year!

Your Word promised us, *I wish above all things that thou mayest prosper and be in health, even as thy soul prospereth.* (3 John 1:2) We believe Your Word. We will be richer this year than in any other year. We will be healthier this year than in any other year. We will have peace this year because we will know You more this year than in any other year!

Your Word further says, *Redeem the time, because the days are evil* (Ephesians 5:16). We recognize that time is Your precious gift to us and it is short. We will be more productive this year than in any other year. We will be more efficient for the Kingdom of God this year than in any other year. We will lead more people to the Lord this year than in any other year. We are unashamed of You and Your Gospel. We will speak Your Word as clearly, as lovingly, and as urgently as possible.

Finally Your Word asks, *When the Son of Man returns, shall He find faith on the earth?* (Luke 18:8). If You, Lord, were to come back this year, I promise that You will find faith on the earth, because I believe You are the Son of God and the soon coming King of the Earth. I believe You shed Your holy blood for the forgiveness of my sins and You rose again from the dead to give me eternal life. I believe You are coming to give justice and right all wrongs. I believe I am serving a Risen, Living Lord who will be with me and my family throughout this year and for all Eternity.

Thank You, dear Heavenly Father, for this New Life in Christ and this New Year to live it in. I pray all this in the Name of Your Son Jesus Christ. Amen.

NEW YEAR PRAYER 2: Individual Prayer

Happy New Year, Heavenly Father! I repent of my sins in _____ (name the previous year), including inward sins of worry and outward sins of distraction and procrastination (name any other weight or sin that needs to be forgiven). I am sowing good seeds and I will reap. I welcome _____ (name the new year) as the Year I reap more than I sowed. You, Lord, call me to be a seed sower and an overcomer.

I confess this is the year the Lord has made, I will rejoice and be glad in it. _____ (name the new year) will be the year we walk into our Promise Land, the year we will be vindicated, lies will be put to silence, enemies will be met with defeat, and justice will bring me supernatural peace. This is the year we will go to _____, _____, _____ (name the cities or countries to go on missions or Bible tour, such as Israel, Saudi Arabia, Thailand, etc.).

Your Word says, *Where there is no vision, the people perish...* (Proverbs 29:18). I have a faith-filled expectation that my goals will be accomplished this year:

My Top Goals

1. _____

2. _____

3. _____

4. _____

5. I will lead someone to Jesus this year.

6. I will make at least 4 disciples this year.

7. I will finish this project God told me to do: _____

8. I will not be adversely affected by any virus or lockdown.

The Lord protects me and calls me His Beloved; He wishes above all things that I prosper and be in health, even as my soul prospers (3 John 1:2). My soul prospers as I seek first the Kingdom of God and His righteousness, therefore I receive a supernatural level of divine healing, financial blessing, and abundant grace. I am blessed and I am going to be an ever greater blessing in Jesus' Name.

NEW YEAR

By faith I declare this is the Season of Harvest and our Time of Vindication: the Lord will build His Church and the gates of hell will not prevail against it. The Lord will justify His people, prophets and leaders such as _____ (name a leader who's been censored, falsely accused or attacked by the ungodly).

I have a vision, a faith-filled expectation, that God will use Discover Church and _____ (name your church) in the End Times. We will have more open doors this year than ever before. We will be approved for all permits, grants, apps, investments, licenses, publications and outreaches. We will reach more people online and offline. We will be a blessing to our neighbors and friends. We will disciple more nations, publish more books, release more videos, and reach a billion souls for Jesus. Lord, show me my part to play.

We pray for the Third Temple to be rebuilt in the Name of Yeshua ha Mashiach (Jesus the Messiah). We *"pray for the peace of Jerusalem: we shall prosper who love thee."* (Psalm 122:6) We pray for people who will suffer through Tribulation to be rescued and delivered from the anti-Christ, and not give up.

Thank You for this New Year, Heavenly Father, in Jesus' Name. Amen.

— prayer —

PROVERBS 29:18 Where there is no vision, the people perish...

For each and every year, write your vision and dreams!

You can write your own New Year's Prayer based on these models, and/or you can pray a Psalm corresponding to the current year.

THE PSALM-YEAR CODE

Psalm 125 predicts peace upon Israel, which is ironically means that there was intense war before. Indeed, Hamas attacked Israel on October 6, 2023 and war has been raging continuously in Israel throughout 2024. My timeline of war continues till the end of 2026, so why does the Psalm that corresponds to 2025 proclaim peace? We will soon find out.

PSALM 125

3 For the scepter of wickedness shall not rest On the LAND allotted to the righteous [Israel], Lest the righteous reach out their hands to iniquity [the reason God will not let the wicked take land in Israel, lest the righteous become wicked].

4 Do good, O Lord, to those who are good, And to those who are upright in their hearts.

5 As for such as turn aside to their crooked ways, The Lord shall lead them away With the workers of iniquity. Peace be upon Israel!

MY CONFESSION for 2025 would be: *"Do good, O Lord, to those of us who are good, but as for crooks, lead them away…far, far away. Let 2025 be marked by a clear distinction between the believers and the doubters, those who are just and those who are unjust, those who are rewarded and those who are punished. Peace be upon the Church and upon Israel!"*

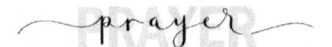

prayer

Psalm 126 is full of joy. It was written about Jews who had been held captive in Babylon for 70 years, finally returning to their Homeland by the edict of Cyrus. It's easy to write a New Year confession based on this Psalm.

PSALM 126

1 When the Lord brought back the captivity of Zion, We were like those who dream.

2 Then our mouth was filled with laughter, And our tongue with singing. Then they said among the nations, "The Lord has done great things for them."

NEW YEAR

3 The Lord has done great things for us, And we are glad.

4 Bring back our captivity, O Lord, As the streams in the South.

5 Those who sow in tears Shall reap in joy.

6 He who continually goes forth weeping, Bearing seed for sowing, Shall doubtless come again with rejoicing, Bringing his sheaves with him.

COMMENT: 2026 may be our last "good year" before the hyperinflation and Global Famine. (See my book about the "*4 Horsemen of the Apocalypse*" for an explanation of the timeline of Revelation.) If this is true, Psalm 127 should say something about a famine. Indeed it does!

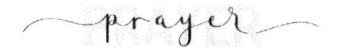

prayer

PSALM 127

1 Unless the Lord builds the house, They labor in VAIN who build it; Unless the Lord guards the city, The watchman stays awake in VAIN.

2 It is VAIN for you to rise up early, To sit up late, To eat the BREAD of SORROWS; For so He gives His beloved SLEEP.

COMMENT: This Psalm predicts vanity, sleepiness, lack of productivity and eating the "bread of sorrows" during 2027. What is the solution to hyperinflation and a crashed economy? Amazingly the next three verses give the answer most people don't see!

3 Behold, children are a heritage from the Lord, The fruit of the womb is a reward.

4 Like arrows in the hand of a warrior, So are the children of one's youth.

5 Happy is the man who has his quiver full of them; They shall not be ashamed, But shall speak with their enemies in the gate.

COMMENT: The solution is babies! The Westernized world is suffering because of a declining youth population and increasing senior population. To keep your nation producing, you must replace the dying and increase the young. Those who will be safe in this time will have obeyed God by marrying, having babies, and raising godly children.

44
PASTORS

Tip: Why should we pray for our pastors? Because the Bible tells us to.

> **1 TIMOTHY 2:1-4** (God's Word) **"First of all, I encourage you to make petitions, prayers, intercessions, and prayers of thanks for all people, for rulers, and for everyone who has authority over us."**

God has an agenda for prayer. There is an order for how to pray. The key phrase is "first of all." We are to pray first of all for our leaders, including our spiritual leaders and their spouses! Then we may pray for our family and our own needs.

Our prayer failures too often come from the fact that we pray first for our needs and a loved one's needs. Follow God's agenda and you will get God's answers.

PRAY: Father, in the Name of Jesus, we pray and confess that the Spirit of the Lord Jesus Christ rests upon Pastor _____, the spirit of wisdom and understanding, the spirit of counsel and might, the spirit of knowledge and of the fear of the Lord. Your Spirit makes him of quick understanding and he will not judge after the sight of his eyes, neither reprove after the hearing of his ears. You, Lord, have anointed and qualified him to preach the Gospel to both the poor and the wealthy, the young and the old, Jews and Gentiles—Americans, Australians, and Asians (name your nationality or people group). You have sent Pastor _____ to heal the sick and the broken-hearted, to preach deliverance to the captives, and recovering of sight to the blind, to set at liberty them that are bruised, and to preach the acceptable year of the Lord.

We pray that no weapon formed against our Pastor shall prosper and that every tongue that shall rise against him in judgment shall be shown to be in the wrong. We pray that You prosper Pastor _____ spiritually, emotionally, intellectually, physically, socially and financially. Shower upon him more grace and favor in Your sight and the sight of man.

Lord, we pray and believe that, every day and in every service, freedom of utterance may be given to Pastor _____ so that he may open his mouth boldly to make known the mystery of the Gospel, that he may speak boldly, as he ought to speak. Thank You, Lord, that You have chosen Pastor _____ and ordained him, that he should bear much fruit (in terms of lost souls saved, sick people healed, empty people filled, disciples made, and all Christians obeying God's Word), and that his fruits should remain!

We hereby confess that we shall stand by our Pastor and undergird him in prayer. We will say only good things that will edify our leader. We will not allow ourselves to yield to a critical spirit, but will continue to pray for him and speak good about and upon him, as is fitting in the Lord. Thank You, dear Lord Jesus, for Your love for Your shepherd. I believe Your eyes are over the righteous and Your ears are open to our prayers! Hallelujah!

Scripture References: Isaiah 11:2-3, Luke 4:18-19, 3 John 1:2, 2 Timothy 1:13-14, Ephesians 6:19-20, John 15:16, 1 Peter 3:12.

PASTORS & MINISTERS who have been influential in my life:

_____

_____

_____

_____

45
PRAISE

A great secret to getting prayers answered is praise. Praise means thanking God for *something*. When you thank God for something He did in the **past**, it requires your *gratitude*. When you praise God for something you expect to see in the **future**, it requires *faith*. Faith praises God before it sees or feels the answer.

PHILIPPIANS 4:6 Be anxious for nothing, but in everything by prayer and supplication, WITH THANKSGIVING, let your requests be made known to God;

COLOSSIANS 4:2 Continue earnestly in prayer, being vigilant in it WITH THANKSGIVING;

The Apostle Paul wrote these instructions while he was in prison. He told Christians living in cities of Philippi and Colossae to pray *with* praise. His circumstances did not deter him from giving praise. Being locked up did not diminish his praise. You could say *because* his praise was in the middle of difficulty, God was moved to shake the earth and break him free from jail.

ACTS 16:25-26 But at midnight Paul and Silas were praying and singing hymns to God, and the prisoners were listening to them. **26** Suddenly there was a great earthquake, so that the foundations of the prison were shaken; and immediately all the doors were opened and everyone's chains were loosed.

PRAISE

Notice Paul and Silas' praise was directly linked to everyone's victory, not only their own! *Every* chain fell off, not only Paul's. Every prisoner got set free by just being next to praise! Praise is powerful.

WHAT SHOULD WE PRAISE GOD FOR?

Victory, for one! Listen to how these four men were all sure of victory *before* anything happened.

1. Moses.

EXODUS 14:13 (KJV) And Moses said unto the people, Fear ye not, stand still, and see the salvation of the LORD, which he will shew to you to day: for the Egyptians whom ye have seen to day, ye shall see them again no more for ever.

The Rea Sea parting was one of the greatest victories of all time. It ended the Israelite's bondage to Egyptian tyrants forever.

2. David.

1 SAMUEL 17:47 (KJV) [David said to Goliath] And all this assembly shall know that the LORD saveth not with sword and spear: for the battle is the LORD'S, and he will give you into our hands.

David's rise out of obscurity started with his defeated of Goliath.

3. A Levite named Jahaziel.

2 CHRONICLES 20:15, 17 He [Jahaziel] said: And he said, "Listen, all you of Judah and you inhabitants of Jerusalem, and you, King Jehoshaphat! Thus says the Lord to you: 'Do not be afraid nor dismayed because of this great multitude, for the battle *is* not yours, but God's.

17 You will not *need* to fight in this *battle*. Position yourselves, stand still and see the salvation of the Lord, who is with you, O Judah and Jerusalem!' Do not fear or be dismayed; tomorrow go out against them, for the Lord *is* with you."

Notice Jahaziel did not need to give Jehoshaphat any further instruction. He knew exactly what to do!

20 So they rose early in the morning and went out into the Wilderness of Tekoa; and as they went out, Jehoshaphat stood and said, "Hear me, O Judah and you inhabitants of Jerusalem: **Believe** in the Lord your God, and you shall be established; **believe** His prophets, and you shall prosper."

STEP 1: Believe the Lord *and* His prophets. Jesus said, "He who receive a prophet in the name of a prophet receives a prophet's reward." One of the prophet's rewards was victory in battle.

21 And when he had consulted with the people, he appointed those who should sing to the Lord, and who **should praise** the beauty of holiness, as they went out before the army and were saying: "Praise the Lord, For His mercy endures forever."

STEP 2: Praise the Lord for His beauty and mercy. That's not easy when you think you're about to get into a big fight and possibly not come out of it alive! Who can think about beauty and mercy? A believer can and will praise the Lord anyway!

22 Now when they began to **sing** and to **praise**, the Lord set ambushes against the people of Ammon, Moab, and Mount Seir, who had come against Judah; and they were **defeated**.

STEP 3: Go out and take action, and watch God fight for you. These "ambushes" are inexplicable. Were they angels? Wild animals? Human enemies turning on each other? The Bible isn't specific about it. It was a supernatural victory because they believed God's Word, sang and praised His beauty and mercy before battle.

4. Messiah.

ISAIAH 61:7 (NLT) [Messiah speaking to His redeemed] Instead of shame and dishonor, you will enjoy a **double** share of **honor**. You will possess a **double** portion of **prosperity** in your land, and everlasting joy will be yours.

(ISV) Instead of your shame you will receive **double**, and instead of disgrace people will shout with joy over your inheritance…'

Praise God for answered prayer before you see it. Praise God for victory!

To see how I praise God in the morning and in the evening, go to the chapters "Morning Praise" and "Sleep."

46
PREGNANCY

Scriptures for Infertile Couples to Conceive and Barren Women to Give Birth

GENESIS 9:1 So God blessed Noah and his sons, and said to them: "Be fruitful and multiply, and fill the earth.

PRAY: *It's a command of God that I am fruitful and multiply, and fill the earth.*

GENESIS 24:60 And they blessed Rebekah and said to her: "Our sister, may you become the mother of thousands of ten thousands; and may your descendants possess the gates of those who hate them."

1 SAMUEL 1:27-28 For this child I prayed, and the LORD has granted me my petition which I asked of Him. **28** Therefore I also have lent him to the LORD; as long as he lives he shall be lent to the LORD." So they worshiped the LORD there.

1 SAMUEL 2:20-21 And Eli [the priest] would bless Elkanah and his wife, and say, "The LORD give you **descendants** from this woman **for the loan** [referring to Samuel whom Hannah vowed to give to the Lord's ministry] that was lent to the LORD." Then they would go to their own home. **21** And the LORD visited Hannah, so that she conceived and bore three sons and two daughters. Meanwhile the child Samuel grew before the LORD.

PSALM 34:10-11 10 The young lions lack and suffer hunger; but those who seek the LORD shall not lack any good thing. **11** Come, you children, listen to me; I will teach you the fear of the LORD.

Tip: Don't be obsessed with the gender of your child. In ancient times, people preferred males because of the first prophecy of the Messiah. God told Satan he would be defeated by the "Seed of a Woman."

God told Adam and Eve the world would be saved by a perfect male born child. Every expectant mother who had a notion of God wondered, "Could my child be the One? I hope he's a boy!" Now that the Messiah has come, we no longer have this high pressured expectation of the male born Savior. Mary has been chosen! There will be no other Mary and no other Jesus.

In the old days, boys grew up to work the farm, and girls grew up to leave the family. But this is no longer as relevant either. So whatever gender your child, please enjoy and love him or her!

NAMES I LIKE FOR MY BABY

BOY NAMES:_____

_____

_____

_____

_____

GIRL NAMES:_____

_____

_____

_____

_____

47
PRIDE

God will protect us from pride and proud people. They are dangerous people and it is Scriptural to pray for protection.

PSALMS 36:11 (KJV) Let not the foot of **pride** come against me, and let not the hand of the wicked remove me.

PSALMS 10:2 (KJV) The wicked in [his] **pride** doth persecute the poor: let them be taken in the devices that they have imagined.

LEVITICUS 26:19 (KJV) And I will break the **pride** of your power; and I will make your heaven as iron, and your earth as brass:

ISAIAH 10:33 ….Those of high stature [like judges, doctors, bankers] will be hewn down. And the **haughty** will be humbled. That's a dangerous use of judicial authority.

ISAIAH 12:11 I will punish the world for its evil, and the wicked for their iniquity; I will halt the arrogance of the **proud** [like social critics, online bullies], and will lay low the haughtiness of the terrible [or tyrants].

ISAIAH 16:6 (KJV) We have heard of the **pride** of Moab; he is very **proud**: even of his haughtiness, and his pride, and his wrath: but his lies shall not be so.

DANIEL 4:37 (KJV) Now I Nebuchadnezzar praise and extol and honour the King of heaven, all whose works [are] truth, and his ways judgment: and those that walk in **pride** he is able to abase.

DANIEL 5:20 (KJV) But when his heart was lifted up, and his mind hardened in **pride**, he was deposed from his kingly throne, and they took his glory from him:

PROVERBS 11:2 (KJV) When **pride** cometh, then cometh shame: but with the lowly is wisdom.

PROVERBS 13:10 (KJV) Only by **pride** cometh contention: but with the well advised is wisdom.

PROVERBS 16:18 (KJV) **Pride** goeth before destruction, and an haughty spirit before a fall.

PROVERBS 29:23 (KJV) A man's **pride** shall bring him low: but honour shall uphold the humble in spirit.

Pride and proud people are a specific kind of enemy. For victory over general enemies, go to the chapter "Enemies." For prayer against tyrants go to the chapter "Protection."

48
PROTECTION

Psalm 91 is the Christian's first stop for protection. I put the entire passage under the chapter "War." Below you'll find more Scriptures for protection against specific things.

PROTECTION FROM DEMONS

MARK 16:17 And these signs will follow those who believe: In My name they will cast out demons

JAMES 4:7 Therefore submit to God. Resist the devil and he will flee from you.

LUKE 10:17 (NIV) The seventy-two returned with joy and said, "Lord, even the demons submit to us in your name."

PROTECTION FROM FAMINE

Please go to the chapter "Famine."

PROTECTION FROM STORMS

MARK 4:39-41 Then He arose and **rebuked the wind**, and said to the sea, **"Peace, be still!"** And the wind ceased and there was a great calm. **40** But

He said to them, "Why are you so fearful? How is it that you have no faith?"

MARK 11:22-24 So Jesus answered and said to them, "Have faith in God. **23** For assuredly, I say to you, whoever **says** to this mountain, '**Be removed** and be cast into the sea,' and does not doubt in his heart, but believes that those things he **says** will be done, he will have whatever he **says**. 24 Therefore I say to you, whatever things you ask when you pray, **believe that you receive** them, and you will have them.

JOHN 14:12 "Most assuredly, I say to you, he who believes in Me, the works that I do he will do also; and **greater works** than these he will do, because I go to My Father."

PROTECTION FROM TERRORISM

2 SAMUEL 22:49 He delivers me from my enemies. You also lift me up above those who rise against me; You have delivered me from the **violent man** [*hamasim*, literally *Hamas men*].

PSALM 140:1, 4 Deliver me, O Lord, from evil men; Preserve me from **violent men** [*Hamas men*]...4 Keep me, O Lord, from the hands of the wicked; Preserve me from **violent men** [*Hamas*].

PROTECTION FROM TYRANTS

LUKE 1:51-52 He has shown strength with His arm; He has scattered the **proud** in the imagination of their hearts. He has put down the **mighty** from their thrones, And exalted the lowly.

DANIEL 4:37 Now I, Nebuchadnezzar, praise and extol and honor the King of heaven, all of whose works are truth, and His ways justice. And those who walk in pride He is able to put down.

JAMES 4:6 But he gives more grace. Therefore it says, 'God opposes the proud but gives grace to the humble.'"

ISAIAH 29:20-21 (CEB) The **tyrant** will be no more, the **mocker** will perish, and all who **plot evil** will be eliminated: **21** all who **incriminate** others wrongly, who **entrap** the judge in the gate, and pointlessly **postpone** justice for the innocent.

PROTECTION

"NO HURT"

LUKE 10:19 Behold, I give unto you power to tread on serpents and scorpions, and over all the power of the enemy: and nothing shall by any means hurt you.

PSALM 121:5-8 The Lord is your keeper; The Lord is your shade at your right hand. **6** The sun shall not strike you by day, Nor the moon by night. **7** The Lord shall preserve you from all evil; He shall preserve your soul. **8** The Lord shall preserve your going out and your coming in From this time forth, and even forevermore.

PSALM 105:15 ...Touch not mine anointed, and do my prophets no harm.

1 CHRONICLES 4:10 (NIV) Jabez cried out to the God of Israel, "Oh, that you would bless me and enlarge my territory! Let your hand be with me, and keep me from harm so that I will be **free from pain.**" And God granted his request.

(NLT) ..."Oh, that you would bless me and expand my territory! Please be with me in all that I do, and **keep me from all trouble and pain!**" And God granted him his request.

GENESIS 26:11 (NIV) [Abimelek ordered his people concerning Abraham] So Abimelek gave orders to all the people: "Anyone who harms this man or his wife shall surely be put to death."

PRAY: *Another blessing of Abraham comes upon me* (Galatians 3:13-14).

JEREMIAH 39:12 [Nebuchadnezzar ordered Nebuzaradan concerning Jeremiah the prophet]

(NIV) Take him and look after him; don't harm him but do for him whatever he asks.

1 JOHN 5:18 (NIV) We know that anyone born of God does not continue to sin; the One who was born of God keeps them safe, and the evil one **cannot harm** them.

ISAIAH 54:17 No weapon formed against you shall prosper, And every tongue which rises against you in judgment You shall condemn. This is the heritage of the servants of the Lord, And their righteousness is from Me," Says the Lord.

PSALM 91:10-11, 15

10 No evil [harm NIV] shall befall you, nor shall any plague come near your dwelling;

11 For He shall give His angels charge over you, to keep you in all your ways.

15 He shall call upon Me, and I will answer him; I will be with him in trouble; I will deliver him and honor him.

PROTECTION FROM WAR

Proceed to the chapter "War."

49
PROPHET'S PRAYER

Adapted from A.W. Tozer's Prayer (1897-1963)

O Lord, I have heard your voice and the fear of God is before my eyes. You have called me to an awesome task in a grave and perilous hour. You are about to shake heaven and earth, the sea and dry land, all nations and Israel, that the things which cannot be shaken may remain (Haggai 2:6, 21, Hebrews 12:26).

O Lord, our Lord, You have stooped to honor me to be Your servant. No man takes this honor upon himself except he who is called of God, just like Aaron was. You have ordained me to be Your messenger to them that are stubborn of heart and hard of hearing. They have rejected You, the Master, and it is not expected that they will receive me, Your servant. My God, I shall not waste time deploring my weakness nor my inadequacy for the task. The responsibility is not mine, but Yours.

You said, "Before you were born I sanctified you; I ordained you a prophet to the nations" (Jer 1:5, 1 Cor 1:30, 2 Cor 1:21). You said, "I will put My words in your mouth, and you shall speak all that I command you (Deut 18:18) and again, "You shall go to all that I send you, and whatever I command you, you shall speak (Jer 1:7)." Who am I to argue with You? You chose me, I did not choose you. You appointed me that I should go and bear fruit, and that my fruit should remain (John 15:16). The decision is not mine, but Yours. Your will, not mine, be done.

It is time for You to work, for the enemy has entered Your pastures and the sheep are torn and scattered. False shepherds abound who deny the danger, and laugh at the perils that surround the flock. The sheep are deceived by these hirelings and follow them with touching loyalty, while the wolf closes in to kill and destroy. I beseech You, give me eyes to detect the presence of the enemy; give me understanding to distinguish the false friend from the true. Give me vision to see and courage to report what I see faithfully. Make my voice so like Your voice that even the sick sheep will recognize it and follow You.

Lord Jesus, I come to You for spiritual preparation. Lay Your hand on me. Anoint me with the oil of a New Testament prophet. Forbid that I should become a religious scribe and lose my dependence on the Holy Spirit. Save me from the curse that lies across the face of the modern clergy: the curse of compromise, of imitation, of professionalism. Save me from judging a church by its size, its popularity, or its offering. Help me to remember that I am a prophet and not a ministry promoter, a prophet and not a man-pleaser. Let me never become a slave to the crowds, or ministry demands or endless emails. Heal my soul of earthly ambitions, and deliver me from the itch of publicity or public attention. Save me from the bondage to things. Let me not waste time puttering around the house. Lay Your terror on me, and drive me to the place of prayer where I may wrestle with principalities and powers, and the rulers of darkness of this age (Eph 6:12, 3:10). Deliver me from overeating or oversleeping. Teach me self-discipline that I may endure hardship as a good soldier of Jesus Christ (2 Tim 2:3).

I accept hard work and small rewards in this life. I ask for no easy place. I deny my flesh, take up my cross daily, and follow You (Luke 9:23). I shall not seek things merely to make life easier. If others seek a smooth path, I will not judge them. I shall expect opposition and try to take it quietly when it comes, trusting in Your grace. And if I should have grateful gifts pressed upon me, stand by me then, and save me from the strings attached and undue obligations that so often follow. And if, in Your permissive will, honor should come to me from Your church, let me not forget in that hour that I am unworthy of the least of Your mercies, and if men knew me as intimately as I know myself, they would withhold their honors and bestow them on others more worthy to receive them.

PROPHET'S PRAYER

And now, O Lord of Heaven and earth, I consecrate my remaining days to You. Let them be many and not few (Psalm 91:16, Deut 6:20, Prov 3:2). Let me stand before kings and rulers as a testimony to them and to the Gentiles (Prov 22:29, Matt 10:18, Luke 211:12); and let me minister to the poor and lowly (Matt 25:40,45, Gal 2:10, James 2:1-4), that I may diffuse the fragrance of Christ in every place (2 Cor 2:15). I am Your servant to do Your will and that will is sweeter to me than position, riches or fame, and I chose it above all things in Heaven and earth. Though I am chosen by You and honored by a high and heavenly calling, let me never forget that I am a man with all the natural faults and passions that plague the race of men. I pray You, therefore, my Lord and Redeemer, save me from myself, and from all the injuries that I may do myself while trying to be a blessing to others. Fill me with the power of the Holy Spirit, and I will go in Your strength and tell of Your righteousness, and Yours alone. I will spread abroad the story of Your redeeming love while my mortal powers endure.

Then, dear Lord, when I am old, have a place ready for me above, and make me to be numbered with Your saints in everlasting glory, in Jesus' Name I pray.

50
PSALM 23

PSALM 23 (NET)

1 The LORD is my shepherd, I lack nothing.

2 He takes me to lush pastures, he leads me to refreshing water.

3 He restores my strength. He leads me down the right paths for the sake of his reputation.

4 Even when I must walk through the darkest valley, I fear no danger, for you are with me; your rod and your staff reassure me.

5 You prepare a feast before me in plain sight of my enemies. You refresh my head with oil; my cup is completely full.

6 Surely your goodness and faithfulness will pursue me all my days, and I will live in the LORD's house for the rest of my life.

51
PSALMS

Psalms is the only book in the Bible that is written to God.* The rest of the Bible is God writing to us. Therefore you could call the Book of Psalms the "Book of Prayers that Get Answered"!

God wrote His laws in the *Torah*, but they would be impotent without His enforcement. Every believer has the right to petition God to enforce His laws on the wicked. To this end, God gave us an entire book to show us how to **pray for justice**: the Book of Psalms!

The New Testament gives us a mandate to use the Psalms just as they are written:

> **EPHESIANS 5:19** Speaking to yourselves in **psalms** and **hymns** and **spiritual songs**, singing and making melody in your heart to the Lord
>
> **COLOSSIANS 3:16** Let the word of Christ dwell in you richly in all wisdom; teaching and admonishing one another in **psalms** and **hymns** and **spiritual songs**, singing with grace in your hearts to the Lord.

With 150 Psalms in total, there is one for almost every occasion. It is

---

* Dane Ortlund, *How the Book of Psalms Is Like No Other Biblical Book*, May 18, 2017, https://www.crossway.org/articles/why-the-book-of-psalms-is-like-no-other-biblical-book/

customary among Jews to recite every day the psalm which corresponds to your age (theoretically when you're 0, you'd have Psalm 1 read to you; when you turn 13, or enter your 14th year, you would begin to say Psalm 14).

Here are my favorite Psalms for justice and peace.

PSALM 9

1 I will praise You, O Lord, with my whole heart; I will tell of all Your marvelous works.

2 I will be glad and rejoice in You; I will sing praise to Your name, O Most High.

3 When my enemies turn back, They shall fall and perish at Your presence.

4 For You have **maintained my right and my cause**; You sat on the throne judging in righteousness.

5 You have rebuked the nations, You have destroyed the wicked; You have blotted out their name forever and ever.

6 O enemy, destructions are finished forever! And you have destroyed cities; Even their memory has perished.

7 But the Lord shall endure forever; He has prepared His throne for judgment.

8 He shall judge the world in righteousness, And He shall administer judgment for the peoples in uprightness.

9 The Lord also will be a refuge for the oppressed, A refuge in times of trouble.

10 And those who know Your name will put their trust in You; For You, Lord, have not forsaken those who seek You.

11 Sing praises to the Lord, who dwells in Zion! Declare His deeds among the people.

12 When He avenges blood, He remembers them; He does not forget the cry of the humble.

13 Have mercy on me, O Lord! Consider my trouble from those who hate me, You who lift me up from the gates of death,

14 That I may tell of all Your praise In the gates of the daughter of Zion. I will rejoice in Your salvation.

15 The nations have sunk down in the pit which they made; In the net which they hid, their own foot is caught.

16 The Lord is known by the judgment He executes; The wicked is snared in the work of his own hands. Meditation. Selah

17 **The wicked shall be turned into hell,** And all the nations that forget God.

[NET] The wicked are turned back and sent to Sheol; this is the destiny of all the nations that ignore God,

18 For the needy shall not always be forgotten; The expectation of the poor shall not perish forever.

19 Arise, O Lord, Do not let man prevail; **Let the nations be judged** in Your sight.

20 Put them in fear, O Lord, That the nations may know themselves to be but men. Selah.

PSALM 31

1 In You, O Lord, I put my trust; Let me never be ashamed; Deliver me in Your righteousness.

2 Bow down Your ear to me, **Deliver me speedily**...

4 Pull me out of the net which they have secretly laid for me, For You are my strength.

5 Into Your hand I commit my spirit...

15 **My times are in Your hand**; Deliver me from the hand of my enemies, And from those who persecute me.

16 Make Your face shine upon Your servant; Save me for Your mercies' sake.

17 Do not let me be ashamed, O Lord, for I have called upon You; Let the wicked be ashamed; Let them be silent in the grave.

18 Let the lying lips be put to silence, Which speak insolent things proudly and contemptuously against the righteous.

19 Oh, **how great is Your goodness**, Which You have laid up for those who fear You...

20 You shall hide them in the secret place of Your presence From the plots of man; You shall keep them secretly in a pavilion From the strife of tongues.

PSALM 54

1 Save me, O God, by Your name, And vindicate me by Your strength.

2 Hear my prayer, O God; Give ear to the words of my mouth.

3 For strangers have risen up against me, And oppressors have sought after my life; They have not set God before them. Selah

4 Behold, God is my helper; The Lord is with those who uphold my life.

5 He will repay my enemies for their evil. Cut them off in Your truth.

[NET] 5 May those who wait to ambush me be repaid for their evil. As a demonstration of your faithfulness, destroy them.

6 I will freely sacrifice to You; I will praise Your name, O Lord, for it is good.

7 For He has delivered me out of all trouble; And my eye has seen its desire upon my enemies.

PSALMS

prayer

PSALM 58

1 Do you indeed speak righteousness, you silent ones? Do you judge uprightly, you sons of men?

2 No, in heart you work wickedness; You weigh out the violence of your hands in the earth.

3 The wicked are estranged from the womb; They go astray as soon as they are born, speaking lies.

4 Their poison is like the poison of a serpent; They are like the deaf cobra that stops its ear,

5 Which will not heed the voice of charmers, Charming ever so skillfully.

6 Break their teeth in their mouth, O God! Break out the fangs of the young lions, O Lord!

7 Let them flow away as waters which run continually; When he bends his bow, Let his arrows be as if cut in pieces.

8 Let them be like a snail which melts away as it goes, Like a stillborn child of a woman, that they may not see the sun.

9 Before your pots can feel the burning thorns, He shall take them away as with a whirlwind, As in His living and burning wrath.

10 The righteous shall rejoice when he sees the vengeance; He shall wash his feet in the blood of the wicked,

11 So that men will say, "**Surely there is a reward for the righteous; Surely He is God who judges in the earth.**"

To find other Psalms in this book:

- Psalm 2, go to the chapter titled "World."
- Psalm 23, see chapter "Psalm 23."
- Psalm 35, see chapter "Assassination."
- Psalm 37, see chapter "Deliverance."
- Psalm 91, see chapter "War."
- Psalm 103, first verses, see chapter "Worship."
- Psalm 144, go to "Leader's Prayer."
- The Psalm-Year Prophetic Code is an interesting subject in the chapter "New Year."

This subject of Psalms is vast and extends beyond the purpose of this book, which is simply to get prayers answered. In a follow up booklet for worshippers, I will explain the Tabernacle of David in a way that I've not heard others say before, the difference between praise and worship, and the distinction between psalms, hymns and spiritual songs. Subscribe to be notified: www.discoverchurch.online

52
QUESTIONS

God Asks Good Questions

Jesus asked great questions.

1. Who do you say that I am? – *Mark 8:27*

2. Do you love me more than these? – *John 21:15*

3. Why did you doubt? – *Matthew 14:31*

4. Does this offend you? – *John 6:61*

There is one question that's foolish to ask:

ECCLESIASTES 7:10 Say not thou, What is the cause that the former days were better than these? For thou dost not enquirer wisely concerning this.

Meaning it's foolish to romanticize the past. People like to say the past was better, but they have bad memories. Politicians and historians romanticize the glory days of empire, such as the period called the *Pax Romana*, a 200-year period starting from about 30B.C. Believe it or not, romanticizing about the past was one of the major reasons for both World Wars!

Every European tyrant has had the *Pax Romana* fantasy of unifying vast territories by force and bringing about a peace that the Bible says did not exist. The *Pax Romana* was precisely the time period in which our Lord Jesus was unjustly treated and crucified, the Jewish Temple was burned, the

Jewish capital sacked, and the Jewish people deported. *Pax Romana* was a time of brutality, torture, mass executions, endless wars and rebellions. Yet dictators will continue to ask the foolish question that cause deaths and suffering, "When can we return to the glory days of the [Roman Empire/ Ottoman Empire/ Chinese Empire/ Japanese Empire]?" Let's ask better questions!

GOOD QUESTIONS TO ASK MYSELF

What mistakes do I want to stop repeating (with God's help)?

_____
_____
_____
_____

How can I improve as a spouse/ parent/ child, etc.?

_____
_____
_____
_____
_____
_____

What are the top priorities God has for me before I go Home?

_____
_____
_____
_____
_____
_____
_____

53
REVIVAL

KEYS TO REVIVAL

In a previous chapter we prayed for church growth; in this chapter we will pray for revival. The difference is that revival affects other churches. When the tide rises, all ships rise together. When revival strikes, other pastors come to learn and other churches grow. The hunger for God overrides the sense of prejudice, fear, suspicion, shame, jealousy or rivalry that keeps pastors apart and congregations isolated.

Pastors begin to visit a church in revival and take back the power of God. Lukewarm churches get on fire. Ordinary Christians pray deeper and worship longer. The entire community experiences more of God in terms of repentance and reconciliation, dreams and visions, healings and miracles.

When enough churches revive and begin to affect the culture, that's an *Awakening*. The United States has only had two Great Awakenings. I am believing for a Third Awakening in our time. There are several promises of this.

ISAIAH 60:2-3

2 For behold, the darkness shall cover the earth, And deep darkness the people; But the Lord will arise over you, And His **glory** will be seen upon you.

3 The Gentiles shall come to your **light**, And kings to the **brightness** of your rising.

PSALM 2:8 Ask of me, and I shall give thee the heathen for thine inheritance, and the uttermost parts of the earth for thy possession. (Mark 16:15, Revelation 5:9).

There are at least 24 keys to revival. Let's touch on 5 of them in this chapter.

1. God promised the whole world—Ask Him for it!

PRAY: *Lord, I ask You for the heathen as my inheritance, and the uttermost parts of the earth for my possession. Make me a light to the Gentiles, bringing salvation to the ends of the Earth (Isaiah 49:6, Acts 13:47).*

2. Persecution

ACTS 11:19-21 (KJV) Now they which were scattered abroad upon the PERSECUTION that arose about Stephen travelled as far as Phoenice, and Cyprus, and Antioch, PREACHING THE WORD to none but unto the Jews only. **20** And some of them were men of Cyprus and Cyrene, which, when they were come to Antioch, spake unto the Grecians, preaching the Lord Jesus. **21** And the hand of the Lord was with them: and a GREAT NUMBER BELIEVED, and TURNED unto the Lord.

I heard a wise preacher say, "*Praying for revival is like praying for persecution.*" Why? Because most Christians aren't ready to make a change till they're oppressed and their freedoms are taken away.

We don't have to pray for persecution. It's coming anyway. But it's possible to pray for revival before the death threats come and drive us to our knees.

3. The Gospel should be accompanied with power, the Holy Spirit, assurance, and good manners.

1 THESSALONIANS 1:5-6 (KJV) For our gospel came not unto you in word only, but also in **power**, and in the **Holy Ghost**, and in much **assurance**; as ye know what **manner of men** we were among you for your sake. And ye became followers of us, and of the LORD, having received the word in much **affliction**, with **joy** of the Holy Ghost:

COMMENT: Some people give up on God when they experience any sort of loss or affliction. They were not assured. They did not learn good manners.

The truth is: we do not understand everything, and we do not admit to everything, and we do not take responsibility for everything. If we did, a lot of losses in our lives would be explainable and reversible. It takes the Holy Spirit and good manners to "receive the word in much affliction" and maintain your joy.

PRAY: *Give us the stamina and good manners when times are tough. We are not God's fair weather friends. We are eternally on God's side. We are forever friends.*

4. All day, all night meetings

ACTS 28:23-24, 30-31 (KJV) And when they [the Jews in Rome] had appointed him a day, there CAME MANY TO HIM into his lodging; to whom he expounded and testified the kingdom of God, persuading them concerning Jesus, both OUT OF THE LAW of MOSES, and OUT OF THE PROPHETS, from morning till evening. **24** And SOME BELIEVED the things which were spoken, and some believed not… **30** And Paul dwelt two whole years in his own hired house, and received ALL THAT CAME IN UNTO HIM, **31** PREACHING the kingdom of God, and TEACHING those things which concern the Lord Jesus Christ, with all confidence, no man forbidding him.

COMMENT: Imagine such a revival that people didn't want to leave the church service. They want to pray, stay, worship, wait on the Lord and receive from the man of God from morning till evening. That's what revival is like!

A balance of God's Word draws people. Paul was able to expound from Moses' laws and the Prophet's visions. He had a balance few preachers have.

PRAY: *Father, let me see this again in my day: church services and Bible studies where people stay from morning to evening. Raise up leaders and laborers who are adept at wielding the Law and the Prophets, handling the Full Gospel without conceit or deceit, proclaiming justice and the end times.*

5. International Missions

Take care of missions. Go where no one has gone.

ROMANS 15:20 (KJV) Yea, so have I strived to preach the gospel, not where Christ was named, lest I should build upon another man's foundation:

PRAY: *Lord, send me!*

LET ME LIVE TO SEE REVIVAL! I WILL DO MY PART BY:

_____
_____
_____
_____
_____
_____
_____
_____
_____

54
SABBATH BLESSING

Every Sabbath Jewish families must rest from their work and come together to enjoy a meal. This meal is typically held after sundown on Friday because the Biblical day starts in the evening, whereas the Gentile day starts in the morning. (Remember the Creation Days of Genesis always started in the evening. "So the evening and the morning were the first day." (Genesis 1:5)

A good explanation for this difference is that, in God, we always move from darkness to light, whereas outside of God, the world always moves from light to darkness. These customs and habits are universal, not dependent on religion; in other words, they are true for all people on Earth, which points to the Bible as the supernatural source of truth above all religions.

Because the Sabbath is a day of worship and rest as a family, practicing Jews tend to live within walking distance from each other. Keeping this one commandment helps families stay together, provides a set time for rest, and reinforces Biblical culture across generations. Isn't God wise?

The New Testament frees us from treating only one day of the week as holy. **"So let no one judge you in food or in drink, or regarding a festival or a new moon or sabbaths, which are a shadow of things to come, but the substance is of Christ."** (Colossians 2:16-17). We can celebrate Christ any day and worship God anywhere. We don't have to go to the Temple of Jerusalem—there isn't one there right now even if we wanted to!

Since the New Testament is a better covenant with better promises than the Old (Hebrews 7:22, 8:6), we should worship God more than the Jews do (once a week) and we should gather corporately in church more than the Jews did in the Temple or synagogue. We should not do less because we are "free." With our freedom in Christ, we should do more than those bound by the Law!

What else do the Jews do that Christians can learn from on the Sabbath? There is a beautiful Jewish tradition on the Sabbath called the blessing of the children. Usually done by the father, with one or both hands upon the children's heads, starting with the oldest to the youngest, here is the blessing to be spoken out loud:

> For boys: "**May you be like Ephraim and Manasseh.**" (The 2 grandsons of Jacob, born through Joseph.)
>
> For girls, "**May you be like Sarah, Rebecca, Rachel and Leah.**" (The 4 matriarchs of the Jewish nation.)
>
> For both boys and girls, the rest of the blessing is: "**May God bless you and protect you. May God show you favor and be gracious to you. May God show you kindness and grant you peace.**"

The question arises why Jewish parents pray for their sons to be like the two great-grandchildren of Abraham, Ephraim and Manasseh, instead of the three main patriarchs Abraham, Isaac and Jacob.

Jewish rabbis have come up with various proposals.

1) Ephraim and Manasseh were the first siblings in the Jewish family who did not treat each other as rivals. Ishmael and Isaac had a rivalry that continues to this day through Islam and Judaism. Esau and Jacob had a rivalry that continues to the present through Arab/ European antisemitism.

The problem with this theory is it doesn't explain why we don't bless boys to be like Abraham? Who was Abraham's sibling rivalry with? (Possibly Haran who, according to the Book of Jubilee, died when Abraham burned his father house of idols, but it's not clear or confirmed by the Bible.)

2) Ephraim and Manasseh were special because they grew up in Egypt, unlike all the patriarchs who grew up in the Promise Land. They learned and practiced their faith in a foreign land and did not succumb to the idolatry of the Egyptians. Now that is a blessing worth passing on to your sons!

I propose a few more reasons.

3) We cannot bless our sons to be like **Abraham** because there is only one Abraham in God's eyes. Even the New Testament singles him out as the "father of faith," "father of all those who believe," and "father of circumcision" (Romans 4:11-12, 16)

4) We would not want to bless our sons to be like **Jacob** or his first **ten sons** because they all had hard lives. Jacob was bereaved of his son, though he wasn't dead. Joseph was rejected by his brothers, sold into slavery, and unjustly cast into prison. Some of the ten brothers had a violent and scandalous past. Yes, repentance and faith finally brought them through, and they learned to accept their brother as their Savior, but their lives could have been much better if they had been more gracious.

5) **Ephraim** and **Manasseh** were the only grandsons of Jacob to be adopted as his own sons. This is a picture of salvation. They were promoted to a higher class, to share in the inheritance of an older generation, not because of any work or merit, but by virtue of being related to Joseph.

This is an object lesson of how to be saved by grace through a relationship with the Messiah. Joseph represents Jesus. Ephraim and Manasseh represent believers who acknowledge they are saved by grace through faith, not by any works lest they should boast.

Ephraim and Manasseh represent the two branches of God's Family: Messianic Jews and Christian believers in Jesus Christ. Thus we pray for our children to succeed not only through their own efforts and merit, but through their relationship with God, the Messiah and us as their parents. They must acknowledge that we who came long before them prepared their blessings. We bless our sons to become recipients of grace and special favor, far beyond what they didn't deserve.

PRAYER

> Let's confess this over our sons: **"May you be like Ephraim and Manasseh."**
>
> Over our daughters: **"May you be like Sarah, Rebecca, Rachel and Leah."**
>
> And over both: **"May God bless you and protect you. May God show you favor and be gracious to you. May God show you kindness and grant you peace."**

I NOTICE UNIQUE BLESSINGS OVER EACH OF MY CHILDREN

_____
_____
_____
_____
_____
_____
_____
_____
_____
_____
_____
_____
_____
_____
_____

55
SEXUAL PURITY

This is a pledge to my own sexual purity.

Explanation: God told me to challenge people to make a personal pledge to sexual purity in 4 areas. Once you read the Scriptures below, you will be able to make the pledge at the bottom with humility and in dependence upon God's grace. He wants you to be fulfilled in every area of life, including socially and sexually.

We must believe He loves us and does not want us to get pregnant out of wedlock, suffer sexually transmitted diseases, or be destroyed by Satan. That's why He tells us...

> **1 CORINTHIANS 6:9-11** (NAS)
>
> **9** Or do you not know that the unrighteous will not inherit the kingdom of God? Do not be deceived; neither fornicators, nor idolaters, nor adulterers, nor effeminate, nor homosexuals,
>
> **10** nor thieves, nor the covetous, nor drunkards, nor revilers, nor swindlers, will inherit the kingdom of God.
>
> **11** Such WERE some of you; but you were WASHED, but you were SANCTIFIED, but you were JUSTIFIED in the name of the Lord Jesus Christ and in the Spirit of our God.

Many early Christians were fornicators, adulterers, lesbians, and sodomites BEFORE they became Christian. But by faith in Christ they were washed [cleansed physically], they were sanctified [cleansed mentally] and they were justified [born again spiritually]. Since freedom for them was possible, freedom for us is possible!

1 CORINTHIANS 6:20 (NKJV) For you were bought at a price; therefore glorify God in your body and in your spirit, which are God's.

There is no question a Christian is called to glorify God in spirit as well as in body. His Lordship is not complete until we surrender to Him our bodies as well as our hearts and minds.

> **MATTHEW 5:27-29** (NIV)
>
> **27** You have heard that it was said, 'Do not commit adultery.'
>
> **28** But I tell you that anyone who looks at a woman lustfully has already committed adultery with her in his heart.
>
> **29** If your right eye causes you to sin, gouge it out and throw it away. It is better for you to lose one part of your body than for your whole body to be thrown into hell.

Jesus said looking with lust is equal to adultery in the heart. Adultery always starts in the mind first. Our English word "pornography" actually comes from the Greek word "pornos" which means fornication and prostitution. Why do these words share the same root? Because fornication, adultery, or any sexual immorality starts with an unchecked thought—a pornographic image. Godly people realize this. That's why in their wisdom they said…

JOB 31:1 (KJV) I made a covenant with mine eyes; why then should I think upon a maid? (NIV) I made a covenant with my eyes not to look lustfully at a girl.

PSALM 101:3 I will set no wicked thing before my eyes…

1 TIMOTHY 5:1-2 (NIV) Treat…older women as mothers, and younger women as sisters, with absolute purity.

SEXUAL PURITY

ROMANS 6:13 (NIV) Do not offer the parts of your body to sin, as instruments of wickedness, but rather offer yourselves to God, as those who have been brought from death to life; and offer the parts of your body to him as instruments of righteousness.

ROMANS 12:1 (KJV) I beseech you therefore, brethren, by the mercies of God, that ye present your bodies a living sacrifice, holy, acceptable unto God, [which is] your reasonable service.(NLT) And so, dear brothers and sisters, I plead with you to give your bodies to God because of all he has done for you. Let them be a living and holy sacrifice--the kind he will find acceptable. This is truly the way to worship him.

GALATIANS 2:20 (KJV) I am crucified with Christ: nevertheless I live; yet not I, but Christ liveth in me: and the life which I now live in the flesh I live by the faith of the Son of God, who loved me, and gave himself for me.

1 CORINTHIANS 6:18 (KJV) Flee fornication.

(NLT) Run from sexual sin!

1 CORINTHIANS 6:14 (NKJ) Do not be unequally yoked together with unbelievers. For what fellowship has righteousness with lawlessness? And what communion has light with darkness? (God's Word) Stop forming inappropriate relationships with unbelievers. Can right and wrong be partners? Can light have anything in common with darkness?

Nothing will stop you from following God's plan faster than dating and marrying an unbeliever. Don't do it! It cost Samson the anointing, his call and his life. Solomon, the wisest man of the Old Testament, lost his passion for God because of all the pagan women he took as wives. Throughout the Book of Proverbs, Wisdom warns us not to fall into the trap of sexual immorality with unbelievers. To live in the center of God's will, to complete your assignment from God, most people will need a Godly life-long spouse. But it is far better not to marry than to marry the wrong person!

1 THESSALONIANS 5:23 (ESV) Now may the God of peace himself sanctify you completely, and may your whole spirit and soul and body be kept blameless at the coming of our Lord Jesus Christ.

prayer

PRAY: *Dear Lord, I surrender my body to You. I pledge to be sexually pure and abstain from these 4 immoral things:*

1 Pornography = adultery of the mind

2 Fornication = pre-marital sex

3 Adultery = unfaithful sex

4 Homosexuality = unnatural sex

When I feel tempted, I will declare that I am crucified with Christ, nevertheless I live; yet not I, but Christ liveth in me: and the life which I now live in the flesh I live by the faith of the Son of God, who loved me, and gave himself for me. I surrender myself to you. (Galatians 2:20)

I flee from sexual temptation like Your servant Joseph did from Potiphar's wife. He was rewarded for his Godly character. In the same way, I ask You to help me keep my whole spirit, soul and body blameless until the coming of our Lord Jesus Christ. Amen.

1 JOHN 4:4 Ye are of God, little children, and have overcome them: because greater is he that is in you, than he that is in the world.

SAY: *Greater is He that is in me than he that is in the world. The Greater One lives in me! He's greater than the lusts in the world. He helps me overcome them. I refuse to take the devil's bait. God inside is my Guide inside. He reminds me that no sin is worth it. God's reward is greater. In Christ, I have the victory!*

I CUT OFF AND RENOUNCE ROOTS OF BITTERNESS that may cause problems for me in my personal life:

_____
_____
_____
_____
_____
_____

56
SLEEP

Good sleep is precious. You can believe for deep sleep.

> **PSALM 127:1-2**
>
> **1** Unless the Lord builds the house, They labor in vain who build it; Unless the Lord guards the city, The watchman stays awake in vain.
>
> **2** It is vain for you to rise up early, To sit up late, To eat the bread of sorrows; For so He gives His beloved SLEEP.

PROVERBS 3:24 (ESV) When you lie down, you will not be afraid; when you lie down, your SLEEP will be sweet.

ECCLESIASTES 5:12 (KJV) The SLEEP of a labouring man is sweet, whether he eat little or much; but the abundance of the rich will not suffer him to sleep.

JEREMIAH 31:26 (KJV) Upon this I awaked, and beheld; and my SLEEP was sweet unto me

PSALM 17:15 (KJV) As for me, I will behold thy face in righteousness: I shall be satisfied, when I awake, with thy likeness.

Every day when I go to bed, my sleep is sweet. My children don't have nightmares. Our family expects to have godly dreams.

What are the Secrets to Good Sleep?

1. Work hard each day.

Solomon said the sleep of a laboring man is sweet. Make your work your worship. Treat God as your boss. Don't do the minimum or the least for Him or His church. Work heartily as unto the Lord and give Him your best (Colossians 1:10, 3:23).

2. Don't eat for at least two hours before you go to sleep.

Don't graze. Don't snack. Don't put junk food or sugar into your body just before you sleep. One effect of sugar before going to bed is it will make you wake you up and go to the toilet several times a night. Coffee or caffeine also affects sleep.

3. Read the Bible before you sleep.

The last thing you see before you sleep is going to affect your night. If you mindlessly scroll through social media while in bed, you will not feel fully rested. If you watch horror shows or scary movies before you sleep, of course it's going to stay in your spirit, disrupt your night, and may give you nightmares.

The world doesn't understand that your spirit never sleeps. When you sleep, only your body is at rest. What is the mind doing? Processing. Its job is to connect the spirit and the body.

If your spirit has a guilty conscience, unresolved anger, hidden fears, or bitterness, your mind will work all night to process those things! No wonder people can't sleep.

I like to go to bed with a clean conscience, having obeyed God and done all that He told me to do. Before I sleep, I've apologized for anything I've done wrong by mistake. I then fill my spirit and my mind with the Word of God.

4. Write down what's important for the next day.

Why is this important?

During sleep your mind wants to process the past and prepare you for the future. The problem is, your mind knows nothing about the future. Your mind is most stressed by the future because it has zero information coming from the future. It only has memories of the past.

So the mind is constantly grasping for things that might give it some control over the future. Data. Guesses. Predictions. Where can it get information about the future? Only from the spirit.

Your spirit is in touch with God if you're a born again Christian. If you're not born again, your spirit has died but you remain an eternal being, so your spirit will still get hunches or "gut feelings" about the future. They're random and not always accurate.

When your spirit is renewed in Christ, fellowship with the Creator becomes normal again with practice. The Holy Spirit can give you precise leadings about the future. This is deeply restful for the mind. According to Jesus, it is one of the Holy Spirit's roles, "He will guide you into all truth…and He will show you things to come." (John 16:13)

So writing down what you believe God wants you to do tomorrow is a very restful exercise.

_____

_____

_____

_____

_____

_____

_____

5. Pray in tongues.

This has the same benefit as above because you're spending time with the Holy Spirit. You are "praying mysteries" which has the same effect as processing the future. Paul wrote about this benefit, "For he that speaketh in an unknown tongue speakers not unto men, but into God: for no man understandeth him; howbeit in the spirit he speaketh MYSTERIES." (1 Corinthians 14:2)

Isaiah described the refreshing benefit of praying in tongues and also predicted people would resist this gift from God: "For with stammering lips and another tongue will he speak to this people. To whom he said, This is the REST wherewith ye may cause the weary to REST; and this is the REFRESHING: yet they would not hear." (Isaiah 28:11-12)

6. Faith.

Believe God wants all His beloved to sleep well. Confess these Scriptures.

PSALM 16:6-7,11 (KJV)

6 The lines are fallen unto me in pleasant places; yea, I have a goodly heritage.

7 I will bless the Lord, who hath given me counsel: my reins also instruct me in the NIGHT seasons.

11 Thou wilt shew me the path of life: in thy presence is fulness of joy; at thy right hand there are pleasures for evermore.

(NIV) **6** The boundary lines have fallen for me in pleasant places; surely I have a delightful inheritance. **7** I will praise the Lord, who counsels me; even at NIGHT my heart instructs me.

(CEV) **7** Even in the darkest NIGHT, your teachings fill my mind.

―*prayer*―

PRAY: *"For so God giveth His beloved sleep. I am His beloved and my sleep is sweet to me. Give me godly dreams and heavenly visions. Work in me that which is profitable to You during my sleep. Speak to my subconscious as my body rests. Instruct me in the middle of the night. When I awake, my flesh will have rested in hope, my heart will rejoice, and my face will be full of joy (Psalm 16:9-11, Acts 2:25-28). I will look and feel younger. I will be satisfied with seeing Your likeness—who is Jesus Christ my Lord."*

57

SOUL-WINNING

ISAIAH 45:14 Thus says the LORD: "The labor of Egypt and merchandise of Cush and of the Sabeans, men of stature, shall come over to you, and they shall be yours; they shall walk behind you, they shall come over in chains; and they shall bow down to you. They will make supplication to you, saying, 'Surely God is in you, and there is no other; there is no other God.'"

PRAY: *Many who encounter me shall be Yours, Lord Jesus. When they see me, they will say, "Surely God is in me, and there is no other; there is no other God."*

ISAIAH 44:24-26

24 Thus says the LORD, your Redeemer, and He who formed you from the womb: "I am the LORD, who makes all things, who stretches out the heavens all alone, who spreads abroad the earth by Myself;

25 Who frustrates the signs of the babblers, and drives diviners mad; who turns wise men backward, and makes their knowledge foolishness;

26 Who confirms the word of His servant, and performs the counsel of His messengers; who says to Jerusalem, 'You shall be inhabited,' to the cities of Judah, 'You shall be built,' and I will raise up her waste places;

PRAY: *God confirms my word spoken as His servant and performs my counsel given as His messenger. I preach the Gospel with power. Those who oppose will be frustrated and sound like babblers. The occult will not work around me, but fortune-tellers and witches will be driven mad by their lack of power. The Lord who made me will be known as the Creator and Redeemer everywhere I go.*

ISAIAH 40:3-6

3 The voice of one crying in the wilderness: "Prepare the way of the LORD; make straight in the desert a highway for our God.

4 Every valley shall be exalted and every mountain and hill brought low; the crooked places shall be made straight and the rough places smooth;

5 The glory of the LORD shall be revealed, and all flesh shall see it together; for the mouth of the LORD has spoken."

6 The voice said, "Cry out!" And he said, "What shall I cry?" "All flesh is grass, and all its loveliness is like the flower of the field.

COMMENT: One of the soul winner's messages is that though life is fleeting, frail and soon passing away, our spirits are eternal and accountable to God. God created us and will hold us responsible for our thoughts, words and actions.

Another simple message of the voice crying in the wilderness is to prepare the way of the Lord; that is, I am to proclaim, "Get ready! Jesus is coming back. Are you ready to meet Jesus?"

ISAIAH 54:2-3 Enlarge the place of your tent, and let them stretch out the curtains of your dwellings; do not spare; Lengthen your cords, and strengthen your stakes. **3** For you shall expand to the right and to the left, and your descendants will inherit the nations, and make the desolate cities inhabited.

PRAY: *My church/ my ministry is growing. We are winning souls locally and internationally. We are expanding to the right and to the left. I have spiritual children who will inherit the nations and turn unbelieving cities into pockets of revival. Praise the Lord!*

You asked me to prepare, to enlarge my tent, to stretch out the limits of my dwellings; I will not spare or hold back. I work to lengthen my cords (evangelistic outreaches, social media, marketing, mission trips) and strengthen my stakes (my foundation, finances, team, staff). To not spare means to not let any obstacle— including finances—hinder me from winning souls. As I build up more soul winners, the Lord takes care of me. I am well paid and pay others well. I treat people, drive people, fly people, take care of people who win souls. Thank God for exponential growth!

PSALM 66:3-5 Say to God, "How awesome are Your works! Through the greatness of Your power your enemies shall submit themselves to You. 4 All the earth shall worship You and sing praises to You; they shall sing praises to Your name." Selah 5 Come and see the works of God; he is awesome in His doing toward the sons of men.

ACTS 16:5 So the churches were strengthened in the faith, and increased in number daily.

WRITE. The names of people I want to be saved this year:

_____
_____
_____
_____
_____
_____
_____
_____
_____
_____
_____
_____
_____

58
STUDIES

Tip: If you're a student, God wants to put you above the rest of the class. You should glorify God in your studies. If you are cramming for 4 hours or more, your brain will get tired and eventually burn out. You are putting too much demand on your brain and under-utilizing your spirit.

There are 2 secrets to passing your exams stress-free. The first is: *it would be far better for you to pray in tongues 1 hour than to study 2 hours or to cram for 4 hours straight.* You will accomplish far more in less time and not feel pressured. Why? Because most stress comes from the unknown, so now is the best time to pray in unknown tongues. You will awaken your spirit, then whatever you "feel" drawn to study will usually be the very questions on the exam. By praying, you tap into your born again spirit which has a larger memory capacity than your brain. The Holy Spirit can also "bring all things to your remembrance" when you tap into your spirit instead of over-loading or over-demanding your brain.

The second secret is to *believe the Scriptures and confess them*. Don't believe what other people think and say about you. They only know your past. God knows your future. Maybe you once were slow, but you're not that way now! You're a new creation in Christ. Find out what God thinks about you because God can change your destiny as long as you will agree with His Word.

One last practical piece of advice about studying: remember that no exam tests you on what is in your head. An exam tests what's in your teacher's head. So be wise enough to pay attention to what your teacher wants to hear for answers. School papers, projects and tests are not designed primarily to reveal your creativity or originality. Those things are given by God, recognized by God, and best used in real life for God. A secular teacher doesn't want to know what's in your head; they want to know if you know what's in their head. So in an assignment or exam, focus on what your teacher knows and repeat those answers back to him or her.

prayer

JAMES 1:5 (NLT)

If any of you lacks wisdom, he should ask God, who gives generously to all without finding fault, and it will be given to him.

PRAY: *Lord, I ask for wisdom and by faith I believe I receive all I need to excel!*

JOSHUA 1:8 (NLT)

Study this Book of Instruction continually. Meditate on it day and night so you will be sure to obey everything written in it. Only then will you prosper and succeed in all you do.

PRAY: *Studying is acting in line with the Word. My studies show my faith in future results. I will prosper and succeed in all I do, in Jesus' Name.*

DANIEL 1:17, 20 (NLT)

17 God gave these four young men an unusual aptitude for understanding every aspect of literature and wisdom. And God gave Daniel the special ability to interpret the meanings of visions and dreams.

20 Whenever the king consulted them in any matter requiring wisdom and balanced judgment, he found them TEN TIMES more capable than any of the magicians and enchanters in his entire kingdom.

(AKJ) **20** And in all matters of wisdom and understanding, that the king inquired of them, he found them TEN TIMES better than all the magicians and astrologers that were in all his realm.

CONFESS: *I am 10 times smarter than my peers because God lives in me! God knows every subject better than my teachers do, and He lives in me!*

PSALM 119:97-100 (NKJV)

97 Oh, how I love Your law! It is my meditation all the day.

98 You, through Your commandments, make me WISER than my enemies; for they are ever with me.

99 I have MORE UNDERSTANDING than all my teachers, for Your testimonies are my meditation.

100 I UNDERSTAND more than the ancients, because I keep Your precepts.

CONFESS: *I am wiser than my enemies and have more understanding than my teachers because I love Your Law. It is my meditation all day long.*

JOHN 14:6 (ASV)

But the Comforter, even the Holy Spirit, whom the Father will send in my name, he shall teach you all things, and bring to your remembrance all that I said unto you.

CONFESS: *I believe in the ministry of the Holy Spirit! I call upon You to teach me and remind me everything I need to know for my exam and success, in Jesus' Name!*

2 CORINTHIANS 2:16b (NKJ) But we have the mind of Christ.

SAY: *I have the mind of Christ.*

1 JOHN 4:4 (NKJV) You are of God, little children, and have overcome them, because He who is in you is greater than he who is in the world.

BOLDLY DECLARE: *Greater is the Teacher in me than the exams, problems and pressures that are in this world. I trust in the Greater One to put me over, in Jesus' Name.*

*Ultimately, we learn because Jesus wants us to be His disciples. What does that mean exactly? It does not mean "believer." The English term comes form the Latin "discipulus," from which we derive the words "discipline" and "pupil." A disciple is a "learner" and a "disciplined person." Jesus wants us to be more than believers; He wants us to be **lifelong learners**. Before every trip you take, take a book with you. Continue to learn every free moment you get. Read before you go to bed.*

STUDIES

BOOKS I PLAN TO READ & STUDY THIS YEAR (one a month minimum)

1. _____

2. _____

3. _____

4. _____

5. _____

6. _____

7. _____

8. _____

9. _____

10. _____

11. _____

12. _____

59
TEMPTATION

Many times I quoted Galatians 2:20 verbatim as a young Christian. This one verse helped me crucify the flesh and overcome a myriad of temptations. It helped me to live a new life aimed to please my Master—Jesus who loved me and gave Himself for me.

> **GALATIANS 2:20** (KJV) I am crucified with Christ: nevertheless I live; yet not I, but Christ liveth in me: and the life which I now live in the flesh I live by the faith of the Son of God, who loved me, and gave himself for me.

1 CORINTHIANS 10:13 (KJV) There hath no temptation taken you but such as is common to man: but God is faithful, who will not suffer you to be tempted above that ye are able; but will with the temptation also make a way to escape, that ye may be able to bear it.

(NET) No trial has overtaken you that is not faced by others. And God is faithful: He will not let you be tried beyond what you are able to bear, but with the trial will also provide a way out so that you may be able to endure it.

HEBREWS 12:2-3 (KJV) Looking unto Jesus the author and finisher of our faith; who for the joy that was set before him endured the cross, despising the shame, and is set down at the right hand of the throne of God. **3** For consider him that **endured** such **contradiction** of sinners against himself, lest ye be wearied and faint in your minds. (CSB) **3** For consider him who **endured** such **hostility** from sinners against himself, so that you won't grow weary and give up.

COMMENT: The secret to overcoming temptation is to think about Jesus. He is not just God in Heaven; He is also God in the flesh—One who cares, can sympathize with our weaknesses, and was in all points tempted as we are, yet without sin. (Hebrews 4:15) Jesus endured so much more than we do. He was tempted with everything, yet He never succumbed. By loving Christ, it is possible to kick temptation and live a life you and He would be proud of. Start making pure and clean decisions one day at a time for Jesus.

ROMANS 8:37 Yet in all these things we are MORE THAN CONQUERORS through Him who loved us. [You're a conqueror—an overcomer!]

1 JOHN 4:4 …Greater is he that is in you, than he that is in the world.

1 JOHN 5:5 Who is he who OVERCOMES the world, but he who believes that Jesus is the Son of God?

REVELATION 3:21 To him who overcomes I will grant to sit with Me on My throne, as I also overcame and sat down with My Father on His throne.

REVELATION 21:7 He who overcomes shall inherit all things, and I will be his God and he shall be My son.

MY STRATEGIES TO FIGHT TEMPTATION

1. **Stay away from danger!** Proverbs 22:3 (ESV) says, *"The prudent sees danger and hides himself, but the simple go on and suffer for it."*

2. **Flee youthful lusts!** 2 Timothy 2:22 says, *"Flee also youthful lusts…"* How do we do that? The rest of the verse tells us to have something worthwhile to pursue: *"…but pursue righteousness, faith, love, peace with those who call on the Lord out of a pure heart."* Verse 23 continues on the same topic, *"But avoid foolish and ignorant disputes…"* meaning philosophy is often a cover up for sin. People get into sideline arguments to distract themselves from the real issue that matters: their life isn't right.

3. **Confess the Scriptures** in this chapter till it's beaten.

4. **Give someone trustworthy** permission to check up on me.

60
WAR

In times of war, distress or conflict, many believers have sought refuge in Psalm 91. Unlike most psalms written by David, Psalms 90 and 91 were written by Moses according to Jewish sages.

PSALM 91:1-16

1 He who dwells in the secret place of the Most High Shall abide under the shadow of the Almighty.

2 I will say of the Lord, "He is my refuge and my fortress; My God, in Him I will trust."

3 Surely He shall deliver you from the snare of the fowler And from the perilous pestilence.

4 He shall cover you with His feathers, And under His wings you shall take refuge; His truth shall be your shield and buckler.

5 You shall not be afraid of the terror by night, Nor of the arrow that flies by day,

6 Nor of the pestilence that walks in darkness, Nor of the destruction that lays waste at noonday.

7 A thousand may fall at your side, And ten thousand at your right hand; But it shall not come near you.

8 Only with your eyes shall you look, And see the reward of the wicked.

9 Because you have made the Lord, who is my refuge, Even the Most High, your dwelling place,

10 No evil shall befall you, Nor shall any plague come near your dwelling;

11 For He shall give His angels charge over you, To keep you in all your ways.

12 In their hands they shall bear you up, Lest you dash your foot against a stone.

13 You shall tread upon the lion and the cobra, The young lion and the serpent you shall trample underfoot.

14 "Because he has set his love upon Me, therefore I will deliver him; I will set him on high, because he has known My name.

15 He shall call upon Me, and I will answer him; I will be with him in trouble; I will deliver him and honor him.

16 With long life I will satisfy him, And show him My salvation."

PREVENTION OF WAR

Better than victory in war is prevention of war.

2 CHRONICLES 17:10 The fear of the LORD fell on all the kingdoms of the lands surrounding Judah, so that they did not go to war against Jehoshaphat.

PHILIPPIANS 4:7 (NIV) And the peace of God, which transcends all understanding, will guard your hearts and your minds in Christ Jesus.

PROVERBS 16:7 When a man's ways please the Lord, He makes even his enemies to be at peace with him. E.g. Esau was at peace with Jacob.

1 KINGS 12:24 [Shemaiah the prophet prevented civil war by telling Rehoboam this] Thus says the LORD, "You must not go up and fight against your relatives the sons of Israel; return every man to his house, for this thing has come from Me."'" So they listened to the word of the LORD, and returned and went their way according to the word of the LORD.

THE LORD FIGHTS FOR ME

2 CHRONICLES 20:17, 29

(KJV) **17** Ye shall not need to fight in this battle: set yourselves, stand ye still, and see the salvation of the LORD with you, O Judah and Jerusalem: fear not, nor be dismayed; to morrow go out against them: for the LORD will be with you.

(NIV) **17 You will not have to fight this battle**. Take up your positions; stand firm and see the deliverance the LORD will give you, Judah and Jerusalem. Do not be afraid; do not be discouraged. Go out to face them tomorrow, and **the LORD will be with you**.

(ISV) **29** Fear of God seized all of the kingdoms in the surrounding territories when they heard that the **LORD had battled Israel's enemies**.

EXODUS 14:13-14, 25

(KJV) **13** And Moses said unto the people, Fear ye not, stand still, and see the salvation of the LORD, which he will shew to you to day: for the Egyptians whom ye have seen to day, ye shall see them again no more for ever.

(NKJ) **14 The Lord will fight for you**, and you shall hold your peace.

(NIV) **25** And the Egyptians said, "Let's get away from the Israelites! **The LORD is fighting for them against Egypt**."

EXODUS 23:27-30

27 "I will send My fear before you, I will cause confusion among all the people to whom you come, and will make all your enemies turn their backs to you.

28 And I will send hornets before you, which shall drive out the Hivite, the Canaanite, and the Hittite from before you.

29 I will not drive them out from before you in one year, lest the land become desolate and the beasts of the field become too numerous for you.

30 Little by little I will drive them out from before you, until you have increased, and you inherit the land.

WAR

prayer

DEUTERONOMY 1:30 (NIV) **The LORD your God**, who is going before you, **will fight for you**, as he did for you in Egypt, before your very eyes

DEUTERONOMY 3:22 (AKJ) You shall not fear them: for the **LORD your God he shall fight for you.**

DEUTERONOMY 7:20 Moreover the Lord your God will send the **hornet** among them until those who are left, who hide themselves from you, are destroyed.

JOSHUA 10:14 (KJV) And there was no day like that before it or after it, that the LORD hearkened unto the voice of a man: for the **LORD fought for Israel**.

JOSHUA 23:3 (NIV) You yourselves have seen everything the LORD your God has done to all these nations for your sake; it was the **LORD your God who fought for you**.

NEHEMIAH 4:20 (NAS) At whatever place you hear the sound of the trumpet, rally to us there. Our **God will fight for us**.

ZECHARIAH 9:14 Then the Lord will be seen over them, And **His arrow will go forth** like lightning.

61
WARFARE PRAYER

Tip: *When I first became a Christian, I wasn't sure how to pray. If you'd like to know how I prayed when I didn't know how to pray, I have 2 secrets for you: 1) praying in tongues, and 2) praying the Warfare Prayer, attributed to "Victor Matthews." I made it my daily habit to pray both these ways before I felt comfortable to converse with God by referring to my own Scriptures. The Warfare Prayer is based on Scriptures and is a great model of prayer.*

Heavenly Father, I bow in worship and praise before you. I cover myself with the blood of the Lord Jesus Christ as my protection. I surrender myself completely and unreservedly in every area of my life to You. I take a stand against all the workings of satan that would hinder me in my prayer life. I address myself only to the True & Living God and refuse any involvement of satan in my prayer.

Satan, I command you, in the Name of Jesus Christ, to leave my presence with all your demons. I bring the blood of the Lord Jesus Christ between you and me.

Heavenly Father, I worship You and give You thanks and praise. I recognize by faith that You are worthy to receive all glory and honor and praise. I renew my allegiance to You and pray that the blessed Holy Spirit would enable me in this time of prayer. I am thankful, Heavenly Father, that You loved me from past eternity and that You sent the Lord Jesus Christ into the world to die as my substitute. I am thankful that the Lord Jesus Christ came as my representative and that through Him You have completely forgiven me; You have given me eternal life; You have made me the righteousness of God in Him so that I am now reconciled. I am thankful that You have made me complete, and that You have offered Yourself to be my daily help and strength.

Heavenly Father, open my eyes that I may see how great You are and how complete Your provision is for this day. I am thankful that the victory the Lord Jesus Christ won for me on the Cross and in His Resurrection has been given to me and that I am seated with the Lord Jesus Christ in the heavenlies. I take my place with Him in the heavenlies and recognize by faith that all wicked spirits and satan himself are trodden under my feet. I declare, therefore, that satan and his wicked spirits are subject to me in the Name of the Lord Jesus Christ.

I am thankful for the Armor You have provided. I put on the Girdle of Truth, the Breastplate of Righteousness and of Love, the Sandals of the Gospel of Peace and the Helmet of Salvation. I lift up the Shield of FAITH against all the fiery darts of the enemy; and I take in my hand the Sword of the Spirit, the Word of God, which is sharper than any two-edged sword, piercing even to the dividing asunder of soul and spirit, discerning between the thoughts of the mind and the intents of the heart. I choose to use Your Word against all the forces of evil in my life. I put on this Armor and live and pray in complete dependence upon You, Blessed Holy Spirit.

I am grateful, Heavenly Father, that the Lord Jesus Christ spoiled all principalities and powers and made a show of them openly and triumphed over them in Himself. I claim all victory for my life today. I reject all the insinuations, and accusations, and temptations of satan. I affirm that the Word of God is true and I choose to live today in the light of God's Word. I choose, Heavenly Father, to live in obedience to You and in fellowship with Yourself. Open my eyes and show me the areas of my life that do not please you. Work in me to cleanse me from all ground that would give satan a foothold against me. I do in every way stand into all that it means to be Your adopted child and I welcome all the ministry of the Holy Spirit.

By faith and in dependence upon You I put off the old man and stand into all victory of the Crucifixion where the Lord Jesus Christ provided cleansing from the old nature. I put on the new man and stand into all victory of the Resurrection and the provision He has made for me to live above sin.

Therefore, today I put off the old nature with its selfishness and I put on the new nature with its love. I put off the old nature with its fear and I put on the new nature with its courage. I put off the old nature with all its deceitful lusts and I put on the new nature with its righteousness, purity and honesty.

In every way I stand into the victory of the Ascension and Glorification of the Lord Jesus Christ, whereby all principalities and powers were made subject to Him. I claim my place in Christ as victorious with Him over all the enemies of my soul. Blessed Holy Spirit, I pray that You would fill me. Come into my life, break down every idol and cast out every foe.

I am thankful, Heavenly Father, for the expression of Your will for my daily life as You have shown me in Your Word. I, therefore, claim all the will of God for today. I am thankful that You have blessed me with all spiritual blessings in heavenly places in Christ Jesus. I am thankful that You have begotten me unto a living hope by the Resurrection of Jesus Christ from the dead. I am thankful that You have made a provision so that today I can live filled with the Spirit of God with love, joy, peace, longsuffering, gentleness, goodness, meekness, faithfulness, and self-control in my life. I recognize this is Your will for me and I therefore reject and resist all the endeavors of satan and his wicked spirits to rob me of the will of God. I refuse in this day to believe my feelings and I hold up the Shield of Faith against all the accusations and distortion and insinuations that satan would put into my mind. I claim the fullness of the will of God for my life.

In the Name of the Lord Jesus Christ, I completely surrender myself to You Heavenly Father, as a living sacrifice. I choose not to be conformed to this world. I choose to be transformed by the renewing of my mind, and I pray that You would show me Your will and enable me to walk in all the fullness of Your will today.

I am thankful, Heavenly Father, that the weapons of my warfare are not carnal but mighty through God to the pulling down of strongholds, to the casting down of imagination and every high thing that exalteth itself against the knowledge of God, and I bring every thought into obedience to the Lord Jesus Christ. Therefore, in my own life today I tear down the strongholds of satan and smash the plans of satan that have been formed against me. I tear down the strongholds of satan against my mind, and I surrender my mind to You, Blessed Holy Spirit. I affirm, Heavenly Father, that You have not given me the spirit of fear but of power, love and a sound mind. I break and smash the strongholds of satan formed against my body today; I give my body to You recognizing that I am Your temple. I rejoice in Your mercy and goodness.

Heavenly Father, I pray that now and through this day You would strengthen and enlighten me; show me the way satan is hindering and tempting and lying and distorting the Truth in my life. Enable me to be the kind of person that would please You. Enable me to be aggressive in prayer and Faith. Enable me to be aggressive mentally, to think about and practice Your Word, and to give You Your rightful place in my life.

Again I cover myself with the blood of the Lord Jesus Christ and pray that You, Blessed Holy Spirit, would bring all the work of the Crucifixion, all the work of the Resurrection, all the work of the Glorification and all the work of the Pentecost into my life today. I surrender myself to You. I refuse to be discouraged. You are the God of all hope. You have proven Your power by resurrecting Jesus Christ from the dead, and I claim in every way this victory over all satanic forces in my life. I pray in the Name of the Lord Jesus Christ with thanksgiving. Amen.

WAYS I'VE CHANGED SINCE PRAYING WARFARE PRAYER

_____

_____

_____

_____

_____

_____

_____

62
WEALTH

The secret to wealth is not luck, winning the lottery, or marrying rich. Wealth is a lot like health. Just as health is generally the result of healthy habits, so too wealth is the result of wealthy habits. What are these wealthy habits? The Bible tells us. It's up to us to learn about them and implement them. Only then will we get results.

The first wealthy habit is to acknowledge we're not the creator or owner of anything; we're temporary stewards. Stewards don't decide how much he gets to keep for himself; the owner does. The Owner of the universe has said that 90% of everything that passes through our hands belong to us, but 10% belongs to Him—called the *tithe*. (Malachi 3:8-12)

There's no point praying for wealth if you're stealing from God. No matter how much money people have, or how many financial miracles they receive, people still struggle to pay their tithes. I've seen multimillionaires cheat God on the tithe and died sick and broke. It wasn't worth it, but the devil tempted them with an un-wealthy habit. Over time, habits form destiny. I would never cheat God and expect it to end well. First, give the tithe to the church you call home. Commit to it for life.

According to God's Word, wealth is a part of the covenant we have with God. Wealth is even a part of the covenant name of God *Jehovah Sabaoth*—the Lord of Armies or the Lord of Hosts. Heaven's Armies fight for the believer who is willing to use wealth for the glory of God.

WEALTH

prayer

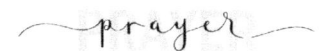

DEUTERONOMY 8:18 "And you shall remember the LORD your God, for it is He who gives you power to get wealth, that He may establish His covenant which He swore to your fathers, as it is this day.

JAMES 5:3-4 Your gold and silver are corroded, and their corrosion will be a witness against you and will eat your flesh like fire. You have heaped up treasure in the last days. 4 Indeed the wages of the laborers who mowed your fields, which you kept back by fraud, cry out; and the cries of the reapers have reached the ears of the Lord of Sabaoth [Lord of Armies or Lord of Hosts].

PRAY: *Dear Lord of Sabaoth, the wicked have stolen from me through seizures, inappropriate government spending, funding unrighteous activities, inflation, exorbitant interest rates, and more coercive and underhanded measures I have never consented to. I am a laborer for God and my wages which have been kept back by fraud. I cry out for justice! Lord of Sabaoth, send Heaven's Armies to release earthly resources so I can accomplish Your great purposes without any financial stress or burden.*

PROVERBS 10:22 (KJV) The blessing of the Lord, it maketh rich, and he addeth no sorrow with it.

PROVERBS 13:22 (KJV) A good man leaveth an inheritance to his children's children: and the wealth of the sinner is laid up for the just.

PRAY: *A good man takes care of his family. I will not only leave an inheritance for my children, I will also have more than enough to leave for my grandchildren. Give me uncommon opportunities and investments. Prosper me with multi-generational wealth. I believe the wealth of the sinner is laid up for us the just. The wealth of this world is being accumulated for the benefit of a man who cares about justice, in Jesus' Name!*

3 JOHN 1:2 (KJV) Beloved, I wish above all things that thou mayest prosper and be in health, even as thy soul prospereth.

JOSHUA 1:3-3 (ESV) Every place that the sole of your foot will tread upon I have given to you, just as I promised to Moses.

TIP: Sometimes a piece of land or a business opportunity will not present itself to you until you travel somewhere. You have to make a move. Why else would God tell Joshua, "Your feet have to touch the ground of the Promise Land"? He didn't say, "Whatever I give you I give you." He said, "Every place that the sole of your foot will tread upon I have given you," meaning you have a part to play. It's not all up to God. You have to travel. Get off your bum! Take a mission trip! Go serve your pastor! Go meet a hero or mentor even if it costs you!

> **GENESIS 26:1, 12-14**
>
> **1** There was a famine in the land, besides the first famine that was in the days of Abraham.
>
> **12** Then Isaac SOWED in that land, and reaped in the same year a hundredfold; and the LORD blessed him.
>
> **13** The man began to prosper, and continued prospering until he became very prosperous;
>
> **14** for he had possessions of flocks and possessions of herds and a great number of servants. So the Philistines envied him.

TIP: Similar to Joshua's example, Isaac had a part to play in the Lord's blessing him. He chose to sow in a time of famine, then the Lord blessed him with a hundredfold when everyone else was lacking. Isaac didn't grow wealthy instantly. There is an element of waiting required every time you sow a seed. Be patient for God to give you the increase.

ISAIAH 49:23 Kings shall be your foster fathers, and their queens your nursing mothers; They shall bow down to you with their faces to the earth, and lick up the dust of your feet. Then you will know that I am the LORD. For they shall not be ashamed who WAIT for Me."

Notice there is no chapter on "Money." I don't pray for money. I tithe, sow, solve problems, cast vision, promote others & build relationships to create wealth. You may wish to pray for "Jobs & Opportunities." To deal with economic recession, see the chapter on "Famine."

WEALTH

WEALTH IDEAS

Write them all down and submit them to the Lord. Wait for His guidance. Not every good opportunity is for me or comes from God.

1. I will never sign my name as a guarantor for anyone else's loan. This violates the Scriptures.

- Proverbs 17:18, "A man lacking in sense pledges And becomes guarantor in the presence of his neighbor."
- Proverbs 11:15, "…he who hates being a guarantor is secure."

The first rule of wealth is don't get into debt for others. Be very careful about taking on financial or legal obligation for others. It's easy to do when you have a good heart; many well-meaning people have lost homes and been ruined by it. Protect your home!

2. I will not act in haste when an opportunity comes.

- Proverbs 21:5, "The plans of the diligent lead surely to abundance, but everyone who is hasty comes only to poverty."
- Proverbs 19:2 (CEB) … rushing feet make mistakes. (NET) …the one who acts hastily makes poor choices. (KJ21) he that maketh haste with his feet sinneth.
- Isaiah 28:16 (KJV) …he that believeth shall not make haste.

Avoid high pressure tactics as they are red flags. Sleep on it for at least 3 days. If you're married, ask your spouse before pulling the trigger. Your first goal in investing is not to make money; it's to not lose your life savings. Invest only what you can afford to lose. Don't trust. Verify!

3. _____

_____

4. _____

_____

5. _____

_____

GET PRAYERS ANSWERED

6. _____
_____

7. _____
_____

8. _____
_____

9. _____
_____

10. _____
_____

11. _____
_____

12. _____
_____

13. _____
_____

14. _____
_____

15. _____
_____

16. _____
_____

17. _____
_____

63
WIFE

When a man is walking in God's will, he is virtually impervious to the devil. When Jesus preached His first sermon in Nazareth, they tried to throw Him off a cliff, but He escaped their hands inexplicably (Luke 4:28-30). When Paul healed a crippled man in Lystra, the crowd stoned him and left him for dead, but he rose up and continued to preach in next town Derbe, then even dared to come back to preach in Lystra (Acts 14)!

If there is one favorite way the devil uses to take down a man, it's through finding his weakest link. That's usually someone close to him, and no one is closer to a married man than his wife. The devil took Adam down through Eve, Samson down through Delilah, and Ahab down through Jezebel.

Most modern churched have been infiltrated by feminism. Christian preachers are thus blinded from acknowledging basic realities about gender. American preachers constantly misquote the Bible and refer to parents as, "Mother and father," when God consistently puts things in this order, "Father and mother." There must be a reason God does that, and a reason American Christians keep ignoring it. There are also consequences.

We need to grasp reality to pray effectively for each other. Abraham was nearly taken out of God's plan by listening to his wife's advice to produce an offspring with Hagar. The whole world is still suffering from the consequences of Sarah's impatience with God's plan for her husband.

> **1 PETER 3:7** Husbands, likewise, dwell with them with understanding, giving honor to the wife, as to the weaker vessel, and as being heirs together of the grace of life, that your prayers may not be hindered.
>
> (HCSB) Husbands, in the same way, live with your wives with an understanding of their weaker nature yet showing them honor as coheirs of the grace of life, so that your prayers will not be hindered.

This is the most important Scripture for husbands to understand. It ties our relationship with our wives to our spiritual health and effectiveness. Wives are the weaker vessel. There is nothing controversial about this unless you're brainwashed and can't see the obvious.

My wife is a pretty strong woman—she lived abroad with tribal people as a missionary, earned an aerospace engineering degree, and managed millions of dollar of property for her family. But my wife will tell you she's weaker than me. If we were in a wrestling match, she would lose.

My wife also feels that I am stronger than she is emotionally. She is a highly capable multi-tasker, yet she feels overwhelmed more easily than I do. She depends on me for stability. She relies on me to make the stressful decisions for our family, especially when her feelings or hormones are fluctuating.

I will assume that if you're a husband who's reading this chapter, you act like the spiritual leader of the home. You make the big decisions, especially for your family's spiritual growth. Of course, there are women who lead and men who follow. This is out of God's order. If a man doesn't lead his family in Bible reading and going to church, I believe he is acting like the weaker vessel. Then this chapter doesn't apply to his wife. It applies to him. He is like Peter before he was "converted" into a leader.

> **LUKE 22:31-32**
>
> 31 And the Lord said, Simon, Simon, behold, Satan hath desired to have you, that he may sift you as wheat: **32** But I have prayed for thee, that thy faith fail not: and when thou art CONVERTED, strengthen thy brethren [i.e. LEAD].

God wants to convert every man into a leader. Since I'm the leader of my home, I accept what the Bible says about who I am, who my wife is, and how I should cover her and pray for her.

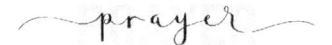

— prayer —

PRAY: *Father, help me to be sensitive to when my wife needs support. When she's tired and drained, let me rise up as her resource and mainstay. Bring godly counselors and helpers into her life so she knows she's not alone. I bind every wrong voice from entering into her mind, in Jesus' Name.*

Help my wife to find balance physically and emotionally, so she can pursue Your plan spiritually. Fill her with the Holy Spirit as she worships and prays, and confirm Your Word with signs following. Help her to fill up with activities she enjoys and cause her to enjoy working towards Your will. Cause her hormones to be stable, her mind to be clear, and her youth to be renewed day by day.

As the head of my house, I call for a wall of protection over my wife and children, in Jesus' Name. Though Satan desires to have them, I pray for them that their faith fail not; and when they are fully converted into leaders, may they have the compassion, motivation and stamina to go on and strengthen other people. When they're tempted to think negatively and see only the problem, open their eyes so that they will see the beauty of Your calling for our family, count our blessings, and be content with what You have given us. Give my wife and children wisdom to convert every negative into positive, in Jesus' Name. Amen.

THINGS I LOVE ABOUT MY WIFE

_____

_____

_____

_____

_____

prayer

5 TOP THINGS THAT FILL HER EMOTIONAL LOVE TANK

_____

_____

_____

_____

_____

_____

_____

_____

_____

_____

_____

_____

_____

Note: *Some women expect men to guess what they want. In a woman's world, this type of assuming shows you care. But for men assuming can be rude. Men don't guess; we follow instructions. We want to be told directly. As a husband, you may be unsure what she wants. It's OK to ask for time to pray for her and hear what the Holy Spirit tells you. He will instruct. (See the chapter on "Future.")*

64
WISDOM

> **JAMES 1:5** If any of you **lack wisdom**, let him **ask of God**, who gives to all liberally and without reproach, and it will be given to him.

Wisdom is one thing you can always ask for. It will come to you in surprising ways. The more I record my life lessons, the more God gives it to me. Here are some nuggets of wisdom God gave me in the early days of my ministry.

1. I am a better friend if I validate, not offend.

JAMES 3:2 For in many things we offend all. If any man offend not in word, the same is a perfect man, and able also to bridle the whole body.

ISAIAH 50:4 The Lord God has given Me the tongue of the learned, That I should know how to speak a word in season to him who is weary

ASK: *What will I do to VALIDATE people's feelings?*

2. I am a wiser leader when I ask, not tell.

MARK 8:27 Who do you say that I am?

ASK: *What QUESTIONS will I ask others to help them discern truth and perceive solutions?*

3. I am a success if I make others' lives better.

1 PETER 4:10 (NIV) Each one should use whatever GIFT he has received to SERVE others, faithfully administering God's grace in its various forms.

GALATIANS 5:13 (ISV) ... through love make it your habit to SERVE one another.

ASK: *Who does the Lord want me to encourage today?*

4. I am a success if I learn.

PROVERBS 4:7 Wisdom is the principal thing; therefore get wisdom: and with all thy getting get understanding.

Everything is a learning experience. No pain is wasted if I learn.

ASK: *What does the Lord want to teach me today?*

5. I am wise if I win souls.

PROVERBS 11:30 The fruit of the righteous is a tree of life, and he who wins souls is wise.

ASK: *Who will I tell about Jesus today?*

6. I am happy if I please God.

LUKE 22:42 ...not my will, but thine, be done.

PRAY: *How can I please You more today? Guide me, dear Lord. What can I do for Jesus today? Speak to me, O Lord!*

After we are born again, God wants to us to grow in wisdom. He wrote an entire book dedicated to it: **Proverbs**! Others have tried to plagiarize or counterfeit Solomon's wisdom, but none of them come close. He wrote 3000 proverbs containing the best advice (1 Kings 4:32).

Proverbs has 31 chapters corresponding to 31 days in a month, therefore some Christians have a habit of reading a chapter a day every month. I don't follow this plan because I would rather complete the Bible each year, but for newbies it would be an easy way to start reading the Bible. When a proverb touches your heart, highlight it and pray for wisdom to do it. Here are examples that touch me.

WISDOM

prayer

PROVERBS 14:34-35 Righteousness exalts a nation, but sin is a reproach to any people. **35** The king's favor is toward a wise servant, but his wrath is against him who causes shame.

PRAY: *"Father, would You exalt our nation with more righteous leaders in the Church, in Congress, in the Courts, and in the schools? Let the King's favor shine towards us. Make us wiser servants for the future of this nation, in Jesus' Name I pray."*

The rest of the Proverbs below are self-explanatory and will make you wise after you confess them regularly.

PROVERBS 15:1-7 A soft answer turns away wrath, but a harsh word stirs up anger. **2** The tongue of the wise uses knowledge rightly, but the mouth of fools pours forth foolishness…**4** A wholesome tongue is a tree of life, but perverseness in it breaks the spirit…**6** In the house of the righteous there is much treasure, but in the revenue of the wicked is trouble. **7** The lips of the wise disperse knowledge, but the heart of the fool does not do so.

PROVERBS 16:3, 7-9 Commit your works to the LORD, and your thoughts will be established…**7** When a man's ways please the LORD, he makes even his enemies to be at peace with him. **8** Better is a little with righteousness, than vast revenues without justice. **9** A man's heart plans his way, but the LORD directs his steps.

PROVERBS 18:14, 24 The spirit of a man will sustain him in sickness, but who can bear a broken spirit? …**24** A man who has friends must himself be friendly, but there is a friend who sticks closer than a brother.

PROVERBS 19:19-21 A man of great wrath will suffer punishment; for if you rescue him, you will have to do it again. **20** Listen to counsel and receive instruction, that you may be wise in your latter days. **21** There are many plans in a man's heart, nevertheless the LORD'S counsel - that will stand.

PROVERBS 22:11, 16, 24-25 He who loves purity of heart and has grace on his lips, the king will be his friend…**16** He who oppresses the poor to increase his riches, and he who gives to the rich, will surely come to poverty…**24** Make no friendship with an angry man, and with a furious man do not go, **25** Lest you learn his ways and set a snare for your soul. **29** Do you see a man who excels in his work?He will stand before kings; He will not stand before unknown men.

MORE WISDOM QUOTES & PROVERBS

65
WORLD

PRAYING FOR THE WHOLE WORLD

God has a Global Reset project. Here are 7 passages of Scripture to believe and confess until they are all fulfilled. They also prove there is no "separation of Church and State" in God's Plan.

ISAIAH 11:9 (KJV) They shall not hurt nor destroy in all my holy mountain: for the earth shall be full of the knowledge of the Lord, as the waters cover the sea.

HABAKKUK 2:14 For the earth shall be filled with the knowledge of the glory of the Lord, as the waters cover the sea.

MATTHEW 24:14 And this gospel of the KINGDOM will be preached in all the world as a witness to all the nations, and then the end will come.

LUKE 10:2 Then He said to them, "The harvest truly is great, but the laborers are few; therefore pray the Lord of the harvest to send out laborers into His harvest."

REVELATION 11:15 Then the seventh angel sounded [the seventh trumpet]: And there were loud voices in heaven, saying, "The kingdoms of this world have become the kingdoms of our Lord and of His Christ, and He shall reign forever and ever!"

GET PRAYERS ANSWERED

prayer

PSALM 2:8-12

1 Why do the nations rage, And the people plot a vain thing?

2 The kings of the earth set themselves, And the rulers take counsel together, Against the Lord and against His Anointed, saying,

3 "Let us break Their bonds in pieces And cast away Their cords from us."

4 He who sits in the heavens shall laugh; The Lord shall hold them in derision.

5 Then He shall speak to them in His wrath, And distress them in His deep displeasure:

6 "Yet I have set My King On My holy hill of Zion."

7 "I will declare the decree: The Lord has said to Me, 'You *are* My Son, Today I have begotten You.

8 Ask of Me, and I will give You The nations for Your inheritance, And the ends of the earth for Your possession.

9 You shall break them with a rod of iron; You shall dash them to pieces like a potter's vessel.'"

10 Now therefore, be wise, O kings; Be instructed, you judges of the earth.

11 Serve the Lord with fear, And rejoice with trembling.

12 Kiss the Son, lest He be angry, And you perish in the way, When His wrath is kindled but a little. Blessed are all those who put their trust in Him.

WORLD

prayer

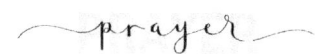

DANIEL 4:17 [Nebuchadnezzar's dream of the tree stump]

17 'This decision is by the decree of the watchers, And the sentence by the word of the holy ones, In order **that the living may know** That the Most High rules in the kingdom of men, Gives it to whomever He will, And sets over it the lowest of men.'

[Daniel's interpretation]

24 this is the interpretation, O king, and this is the decree of the Most High, which has come upon my lord the king:

25 They shall drive you from men, your dwelling shall be with the beasts of the field, and they shall make you eat grass like oxen. They shall wet you with the dew of heaven, and seven times shall pass over you, **till you know** that the Most High rules in the kingdom of men, and gives it to whomever He chooses.

26 "And inasmuch as they gave the command to leave the stump and roots of the tree, your kingdom shall be assured to you, **after you come to know** that Heaven rules.

32 And they shall drive you from men, and your dwelling shall be with the beasts of the field. They shall make you eat grass like oxen; and seven times shall pass over you, **until you know** that the Most High rules in the kingdom of men, and gives it to whomever He chooses."

66
WORSHIP

PSALM 103

1 Bless the Lord, O my soul; And all that is within me, bless His holy name!

2 Bless the Lord, O my soul, And forget not all His benefits:

3 Who forgives all your iniquities, Who heals all your diseases,

4 Who redeems your life from destruction, Who crowns you with lovingkindness and tender mercies,

5 Who satisfies your mouth with good things, So that your youth is renewed like the eagle's.

6 The Lord executes righteousness And justice for all who are oppressed.

PSALM 22:3 (KJV) But thou art holy, O thou that inhabitest the praises of Israel. (NASB 1995) Yet You are holy, O You who are enthroned upon the praises of Israel.

PSALM 100:4 Enter into His gates with thanksgiving, And into His courts with praise. Be thankful to Him, and bless His name.

WORSHIP

PSALM 34:1-8

1 I will bless the Lord at all times; His praise shall continually be in my mouth.

2 My soul shall make its boast in the Lord; The humble shall hear of it and be glad.

3 Oh, magnify the Lord with me, And let us exalt His name together.

4 I sought the Lord, and He heard me, And delivered me from all my fears.

5 They looked to Him and were radiant, And their faces were not ashamed.

6 This poor man cried out, and the Lord heard him, And saved him out of all his troubles.

7 The angel of the Lord encamps all around those who fear Him, And delivers them.

8 Oh, taste and see that the Lord is good; Blessed is the man who trusts in Him!

JOHN 4:23-24 But the hour is coming, and now is, when the true worshipers will worship the Father in spirit and truth; for the Father is seeking such to worship Him. God is Spirit, and those who worship Him must worship in spirit and truth."

HEBREWS 13:15 Therefore by Him let us continually offer the sacrifice of praise to God, that is, the fruit of our lips, giving thanks to His name.

COLOSSIANS 3:16 Let the word of Christ dwell in you richly in all wisdom, teaching and admonishing one another in **psalms** and **hymns** and **spiritual songs**, singing with grace in your hearts to the Lord."

PSALM 29:2 Give unto the Lord the glory due to His name; Worship the Lord in the BEAUTY of holiness.

PSALM 63:3-4 Because Your lovingkindness is better than life, My lips shall praise You. Thus I will bless You while I live; I will lift up my hands in Your name.

PSALM 95:6,9 Oh come, let us worship and bow down; Let us kneel before the Lord our Maker... **9** Oh, worship the Lord in the BEAUTY of holiness! Tremble before Him, all the earth.

PSALM 138:2 I will worship toward Your holy temple, And praise Your name For Your lovingkindness and Your truth; For You have magnified Your WORD above all Your NAME."

COMMENT: Let that sink in! Jesus' Name is the only one we must call on to be saved. Jesus' Name is the only one that makes demons flee. Yet God has exalted His Word above His Name.

SAY: *Thank You, Lord, for Your Word. Your Word is high and lifted up! Your Word is true and living! Your Word is everlasting!*

PSALM 145:3 Great is the Lord, and greatly to be praised; And His greatness is unsearchable.

PSALM 148:13 Let them praise the name of the Lord, For His name alone is exalted; His glory is above the earth and heaven."

PSALM 150:2,6 Praise Him for His mighty acts; Praise Him according to His excellent greatness!... **6** Let everything that has breath praise the Lord. Praise the Lord!

ISAIAH 6:3 And one cried to another and said: 'Holy, holy, holy is the Lord of hosts; The whole earth is full of His glory!'

1 CHRONICLES 16:29 GIVE to the Lord the GLORY due His name; Bring an OFFERING, and come before Him. Oh, worship the Lord in the BEAUTY of holiness!

COMMENT: Notice David's instructions in this psalm, *"Bring an offering!"* We should not come before the Lord empty-handed. This is so important this entire song is repeated in Psalm 105. An offering gives God glory. **Giving** is a big part of worship.

REVELATION 4:8 (KJV) And the four beasts had each of them six wings about him; and they were full of eyes within: and they rest not day and night, saying, Holy, holy, holy, Lord God Almighty, which was, and is, and is to come.

REVELATION 4:11 [How the 24 elders in the Throne Room of God worshipped] You are worthy, O Lord, To receive glory and honor and power; For You created all things, And by Your will they exist and were created.

PHILIPPIANS 2:9-11 Therefore God also has highly exalted Him [Jesus] and given Him the name which is above every name, that at the name of Jesus every knee should bow, of those in heaven, and of those on earth, and of those under the earth, and that every tongue should confess that Jesus Christ is Lord, to the glory of God the Father.

The first act of worship in anyone's life is recognizing God's Name. The very moment we worship Jesus' Name for who He truly is—not merely a religious teacher or leader, but the divine Son of God who walked perfectly on the earth, the only sinless Savior who died for our sins, the only Hero who defeated death—at that moment of worship, we are *saved*.

SAY: *I worship You Lord Jesus Christ, Son of God, Sinless Savior. Forgive me all my sins. I call on the Name of Jesus and I am saved.*

LUKE 2:14 (ESV) [Angels sang] "Glory to God in the highest, and on earth peace among those with whom he is pleased."

MEET STEVE CIOCCOLANTI

Steve Cioccolanti, B.A., M.Ed., is a six-time #1 Best-selling author on Amazon. With over 60 million views, he is one of the most watched Christian YouTubers worldwide and is known as "YouTube's Favorite Pastor."

Watch and subscribe here:
www.YouTube.com/DiscoverMinistries

Born in Thailand to a family of Buddhists, Catholics, Methodists, and Muslims, Cioccolanti has a unique perspective and practical insights into spiritual life. He leads an international church and ministry in Melbourne, Australia and Florida, USA.

Having travelled to more than 50 nations, Cioccolanti is a sought after speaker on end-time prophecy, Biblical justice, world religions and breaking news from a Christian perspective. He is currently authoring more books, filming more videos, and sharing Biblical truths around the world.

Join Online Church!
www.DiscoverChurch.online

Discover Partners Club
www.DiscoverChurch.Online/partner

Partner Internationally with Discover Ministries
www.Discover.org.au/Give

To book Pastor Steve Cioccolanti for your church or event, contact:
info@discover.org.au

Connect with Steve Cioccolanti on social media:

facebook.com/discoverministry
x.com/cioccolanti
patreon.com/cioccolanti
amazon.com/author/newyorktimesbestseller

MORE BESTSELLERS
BY THE PUBLISHER

THE DIVINE CODE:
A Prophetic Encyclopedia of Numbers
VOLUME I (1 to 25)
VOLUME II (26 to 1000)

FOREWORD BY WAYNE CORDEIRO

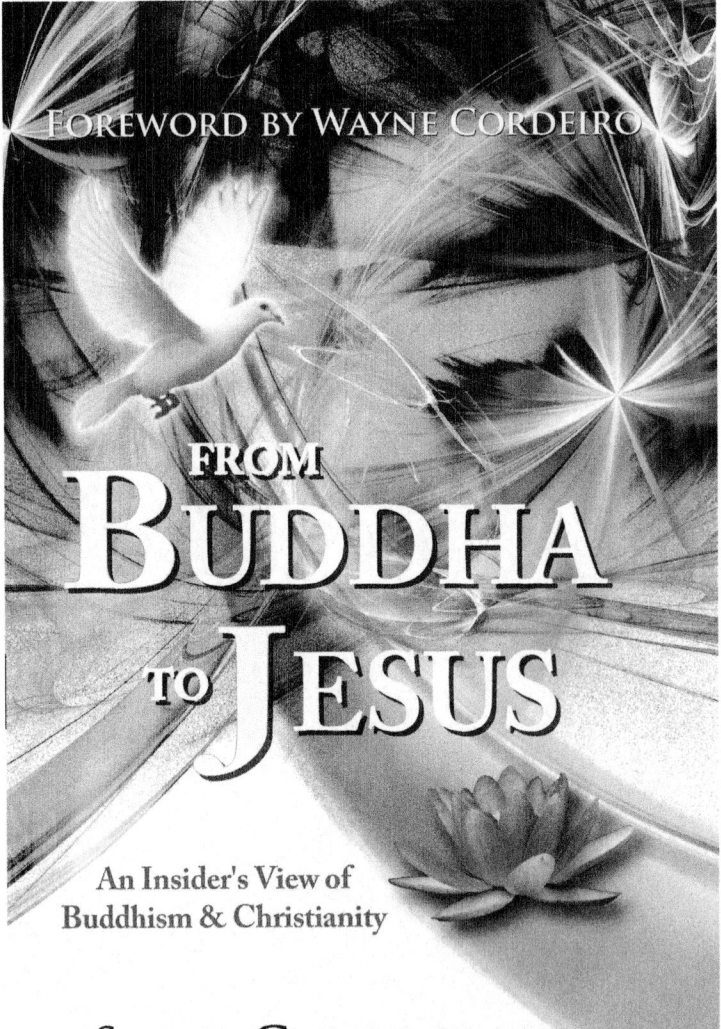

FROM BUDDHA TO JESUS

An Insider's View of
Buddhism & Christianity

STEVE CIOCCOLANTI

From BUDDHA to JESUS
(in English, Cambodian, Chinese, French,
Hebrew, Indonesian, Japanese and Thai)
#1 Bestseller in Asia
by Pastor Steve Cioccolanti

30 Days to a New You
(A Compact Plan for Personal Growth)

Scam Proof Your Life in the End Times (100 pages)
(Paperback or Kindle)

All e-books available through Google Play or Amazon.com/author/newyorktimesbestseller

HOLY SPIRIT LEADINGS

Share your answered prayers at discoverchurch.online

"He will guide you into all truth…He will tell you things to come." John 16:13

"Write the vision…That he may run who reads it." Habakkuk 2:2

MY MUST DO'S

MY MUST DO'S

"Write the vision…That he may run who reads it." Habakkuk 2:2

MY MUST DO'S

MY MUST DO'S

"Write the vision…That he may run who reads it." Habakkuk 2:2

Printed in Great Britain
by Amazon